C#

A Comprehensive Beginners Guide to Learn C# Programming from A - Z.

TABLE OF CONTENTS

Chapter One: Basic Introduction to the C Sharp Programming Language. 1

Introduction.. 1

Objectives of this Chapter 2

What is Programming? 2

Importance of Programming 3

Definition 4

    The C# Language.. 4

    The Dot Net Framework/Platform 5

Keywords 6

Elements of the C sharp language............................. 7

Basics of the C# Language 8

    The overall format of a C# Program 8

Defining and Exploring of Classes............................. 9

Parts of a Class.. 10

    Methods 10

    Constructors 11

    Finalizer 12

    Properties 13

    Indexer.. 14

    Events 15

    Operators.. 15

Structures..15

Static Classes...16

Nested Classes 17

Examples of simple C sharp program 18

The definition of the C# class...19

The definition of the C# Method 19

The Contents of the Method 20

Understanding Our Example 2..21

Practical Questions 24

SUMMARY OF THE C# LANGUAGE.. 24

Exercises... 25

Points to Note. 26

Chapter Two: The Dot Net (.NET) Structure in C sharp language ... 28

Introduction 28

Background Information on the Dot Net platform..................28

The Dot Net Technologies..29

Developing console programs 31

Input..31

Errors...32

Command line arguments.. 33

Advanced Operations.. 37

Inheritance 37

Interfacing 40

Abstract Classes 42

Partial classes 45

Object Lifetime..46

The Garbage Collector... 47

Chapter Three: Existence of various Data Types, Constants and Variables in C sharp Programming Language 51

Data types... 51

    What are Data types?.. 51

    Integer types.. 53

    Character type 57

    String type 58

    Object type 58

Nullable Data Types... 59

    Understanding our code;.. 60

Variables 60

Summary.. 65

Chapter Four: Data Structures, Handling and Functions.................67

Introduction and Significance of Data Structures 67

Enumerations, Arrays and structs 68

    Enumerations 68

    Arrays.. 69

    Structs... 69

When to choose a data structure.. 72

    Array 72

    Dynamic Arrays.. 73

    Linked lists 74

    Stack 74

    Queue 75

    Hash table (Dictionary Implementation)................................ 75

Hash table (Set implementation)..76

Balance Tree (Dictionary Implementation) 76

Balance tree (Set implementation)..77

Practical Example of choice of a Data Structure......................... 77

Summary (How to choose an appropriate Data structure).......... 86

Chapter Five: Control Statements, Loops and Conditions............. 88

Introduction 88

Definition of other statements in C# Programming language.89

Control Statements...89

Conditional statements...90

The If Statement 90

Switch Statement...92

Looping Statements 93

The While loop..94

The Do-while loop..96

The For-loop...97

The Foreach-loop 99

The Nested Loops...100

Chapter Six: Arrays in C Sharp Programming Language.................102

Definition 102

Declaration and Allocating declared Arrays 103

Declaration of an Array..103

Creating an Array 103

Initialization of Arrays and Allocation of Default Values.......104

Boundaries of the Array.. 104

Traversing the Boundaries of an Array 105

Identification of Arrays (Reading of Arrays)................................107

Printing an Array to the Display 109

Multidimensional types of arrays................................109

Definition of Matrices... 110

Declaring and Allocation of Multi-dimensional Array........... 110

Initializing a 2-Dimensional Array................................ 111

Multi-dimensional Arrays Length 112

Arrays of arrays 113

Declaring and Allocating Memory to Jagged Arrays 113

Allocation of Memory to Jagged Arrays 114

Access to the components 114

Practical exercises 115

Chapter Seven: Methods and Recursions 117

Definition and importance of methods......................................117

What is the importance of methods? 118

Declaration and implementation of methods..........................119

The method signature 120

The Method Names... 121

The Method's Body 122

Practical Exercises 123

Recursion 123

Types of recursions.. 125

Creation of Recursive methods 126

Practical Exercises 128

Chapter Eight: Application of Graphical User Interface.................129

The Graphical Hardware and Software..................................... 130

    The Graphic Hardware 130

    Graphical software...131

Practical Exercise... 134

Chapter Nine: Basic Introduction of Lambda Expression 138

Body of Lambda Expressions 140

Practical Exercise.. 141

Chapter Ten: Object-Oriented Programming 142

Introduction 142

Introduction to classes, objects and namespaces 142

Relationship between C sharp programming language and OOP143

Practical exercise 148

Definition and fundamental principles (Inheritance, Abstraction,

    Polymorphism and Encapsulation) 151

    Inheritance...152

    Abstraction...154

    Encapsulation...155

    Polymorphism 156

Practical Exercises 157

Chapter Eleven: Summary and Conclusion 158

Have you solved all the problems?.. 158

What next after this book? 159

Chapter One

Basic Introduction to the C Sharp Programming Language.

Introduction

Over the years, many languages have been developed and manipulated to achieve specific tasks. The classification of these languages depends on the level of use and the complexity involved in dealing with the language. These languages can either be low-level languages or high-level languages.

In the radical world, numerous high-level languages have emerged and developed. These languages have turned out to be commercially lucrative in terms of manipulation. In most cases, the modules of the high-level programming use the concepts in C# language for the purpose of their development.

The C# language was initiated and developed by Microsoft together with the introduction of the Dot Net Interface. The combination of the two inventions forms a runtime supporting environment. This makes the experience of a high-level language to be very interesting and easy to come up with fascinating complicated programs.

Objectives of this Chapter

In this chapter we are going to emphasize on the introduction to basic programming as related to the C# language. We will teach ourselves how to go about this language and write programs. We will familiarize with the language and tackle each and every part of the language. This will entail using simple and reliable techniques that will help us understand the language with a lot of ease.

In addition, we will study the Dot Net Framework as well as the terminology that goes along with the C# language. We will also examine and study the tools that are used in the programming of the C# language. We will write simple programs using the C# language and examine each and every part of the program to know what each role plays. Besides, we will compile and run the codes from Microsoft visual studio as we refer to the MSDN library. This is basically the library that houses the documentation part of the Dot Net Platform.

What is Programming?

In the modern world, computers have become the solution to each and every problem in almost all situations. They are used to control, apply and simulate all the operations in most of the programs. Many tend to forget that the applications that are running in those computers are a result of intelligent background programming. It is important to know that behind the smart programming must be through the use of a programming language. This leads us to ask ourselves the question "what is programming?"

Programming is the means and technique of writing sequential instructions or a sequence of instructions that work to command a computer to achieve a special command. The sequential instructions that are given to the computer are referred to as "computer programs" or "computer scripts"

Importance of Programming

Many may ask themselves about the essence of programming and eventually fail to understand its importance. The importance of programming is to majorly control the working of a computer in order to output accurate and expected results. This is achieved by the correct issue of commands by the programmer.

For efficient programming, the programmer has to be organized and smart in coding the sequence of instructions. The coding of the sequential instructions are usually in written format and the computer follows the instructions to perform each and every step during an instruction. It is important to note that programming utilizes the concept of algorithms which include solving a problem by use of defined steps.

In addition, the method of programming utilizes different languages that are available to make sure the end product is exactly what was intended. It is vital to understand that each and every programming language tends to control the computer to another different level. The languages are either coordinated towards the machine level or the system level.

Before learning more of the C# language and its programming techniques, it is prudent that we remind ourselves of the software or program development. There are different stages that are included and we shall mention them briefly.

The stages include;

i) **Grouping and collecting** information about what is needed before undertaking the task.

ii) **Planning, preparing and scheming** the design or architectural plan.

iii) **Implementing** the scheme which includes the coding of the sequence of instructions.

iv) **Running and testing** the codes or instructions.

v) **Debugging, exploitation and deployment** of the program.

vi) **Support**.

Note: The last three stages of the program development are usually accomplished by programming.

Definition

The C# Language

The language is commonly referred to as the "SEE SHARP". It is a multi-purpose programming language that is suitable and adjustable to the trending and developing modern world.

The language was initially derived from the popular C Programming language. A new feature was discovered in the C# language that was known as garbage collection that made the language more superior to the mother language (C language) and the C++ language. The language also has features that are similar to other high-level languages such as an extensive library, exceptional handling, polymorphism and

4

separation of interface from the actual implementations. In summary, the combination of all those sophisticated features and its powerful development support tools make the language very efficient and proficient in the development of software and other related projects. The language shares many features with the Java Language.

In addition, the language can be used in projects like; radical application projects, internet applications and generally projects that require very strict reliable characteristics. The language is also able to be applied in the testing of frameworks such as NUnit. This is because it has a strong typing procedure that helps to prevent programmers from making errors that are consistent in weak typing languages. In summary, the language proves to be the best in Extreme Programming (XP) cases.

The Dot Net Framework/Platform

We are going to have a brief overview of the Dot Net Platform because it will be discussed in the later chapters.

The Dot Net platform consists of the C# language, auxiliary, libraries and the CLR. This platform consists of the following versions;

– **Dot Net Framework-** this is the most common version that is usually available for general purposes. It is majorly used in the development of applications such as windows, console and web applications using a graphical user interface.

– **Dot Net Compact Framework-** this is a summarized version of the standard framework and is mostly used in the making of mobile phones applications.

- **Silverlight**-is also a summarized version of the original but is intended for used by web browsers to implement complex internet operations.

- **Dot Net for Windows Store applications**- is a small section of the framework that was designed for execution of Dot Net apps in Windows RT and Windows 8 environment.

It is important to note that programs that are developed using Dot Net usually need a virtual machine that can run perfectly on a host. The virtual machine is usually referred to as Common Language Runtime (CLR)

The detailed discussion about this platform/framework will be discussed comprehensively in the next chapter.

Keywords

- **Algorithm**- these are a group of sequential steps that are used to achieve and complete a task and observe an expected output.

- **Programmers**- these are the people that create a sequence of instructions that command a computer to achieve a specific action.

- **Compilers**-these are special programs that change computer programming language from human readable to computer readable format.

- **Syntax**- this is the correct format for each component of the C# programming language.

- **IDE**-(Integrated Development Environment). This is a platform where the programmer conducts all different collective tasks under a single program rather than opening different programs. Examples of IDEs include: Visual Basic, Visual Studio, Visual C# and Visual Web Developer.

- **Identifier**- these are the names that are used in a programming language.

- **Constants**- these are a variety of data in a program that stays the same throughout the whole program.

- **Variables**- these are a variety of quantities that change during the execution of a program.

- **Namespaces and classes**- the namespace can be described as the space in which the code will dwell in. Classes can be simply described as the blueprints of how objects in a programming language will define their concept of operation.

Elements of the C sharp language

The output product of the C# compiler is usually referred to as the "Assembly". It is usually terminated with an extension of ".dll" or ".exe". They usually run on the CLR and are very different from a native coding that may be ending with the same ".exe"

The C# has two types of applications which include;

A. **Console Application**- the console application runs in the computer command prompt.

B. **Windows Application**- this application runs in the computer window and it utilizes the Graphical User Interface.

7

Basics of the C# Language

- **Naming Conventions**- this describes the accepted standards of naming in C#

- **Variables**-This is used in storing data of various shapes.

- **Syntax**-Describes the interpretations of the written applications

- **Data structures**- these are enumerations and structs that are used

- **Exceptions**- these are features of response to errors that may emerge.

- **Control statements**- these include; loops and conditions that govern the flow of the program

- **Operators**- this gives a summary of the operators that can be used in the C# language such as the "-"for subtraction or "+" for addition.

The overall format of a C# Program

```
prologue comment [optional]
using directive
namespace
{
class
  {
functions [optional]
Main function
    {
declarations [optional]
Main function body
    }
  }
}
```

Defining and Exploring of Classes

Just as other object-oriented languages, C# language is implemented using the class criterion. The characteristics, properties and methods of any class are defined by the coding that also manages the behavior of the same class.

The C# classes work in various capacities to achieve different properties. For instance, it performs encapsulation to achieve information hiding in its methods and properties. This is made efficient by enabling different kinds of polymorphism such as subtyping polymorphism and parametric polymorphism. These polymorphisms are done through inheritance and generics respectively.

The classes in C# language can be identified and defined as standard classes, static classes, instance classes and structures.

The keyword that defines a class is basically "class" which is followed by the name of the class. The keyword that defines the class instance is "new" followed by the identifier name of the class. The code below shows a class called Manager with properties Number and Name containing empty methods GetPayRoll() and Daily Work(). It is also an illustration of a class instance that uses a Manager class;

```
public class Manager
{
    private string _number;
    private int _name;
    public string Number

    {
    set { _number = value; }
    get { return _number; }
    }
```

```
public int Name
{
    set { _name = value; }
    get { return _name; }
}
    public void GetPayRoll()
    {

    }
    public void DailyWork()
    {

    }
}
public class Sample
{
public static void Main()
    {
        Employee Marissa = new Manager();
        Marissa.DailyWork();
        Marissa.GetPayRoll();
    }
}
```

Parts of a Class

Methods

These are a member of a class that contains some coding. It contains parameters and a list of return values which also contain generic declaration types. Methods can either be static or instance. On the static side, it is associated, accessed and related through the class. On the other end, the instance method is accessed and associated via an object instance. The instance of the object is that of the same class.

Constructors

They are majorly used in controlling the initial part of a class. The codes of the constructors usually execute the initialization part of the class instance upon the request of a program for a new object. Constructors are not restricted to their functions but they usually set properties or characteristics of the reference class.

Constructors do share similar characteristics with methods. For instance, they also have parameters. For a person to create an object by utilizing constructors, they have to touch on the parameters. This is because the new commands will only accept the constructors that have the parameters.

The example below illustrates the concept of parameters. There is a definition and instantiation of multiple objects from the Manager class;

```
public class Manager
{
public Manager()
    {
        System.Console.WriteLine("Constructed not having parameters");
    }
public Manager(string text)
    {
        System.Console.WriteLine(text);
    }
}
public class Sample
{
    public static void Main()
    {
        System.Console.WriteLine("Start");
        Manager Gloria = new Manager();
        Manager Kenny = new Manager("Parameter equating
```

construction");
```
        System.Console.WriteLine("End");
    }
}
```

The resultant output will be:

Start
Constructed having parameters
Parameter equating construction
End

Finalizer

They are sometimes defined as the antonyms (Opposites) of the constructors. They dictate the final operational behavior of the object when it is not in use. In the past, they were used by the C++ language to free their memories but they are no longer in use in the C# language. This is because the Dot Net framework introduced a garbage collector that usually frees up the memory.

The Finalizer has no parameters. It is usually referenced when the object is no longer called. The Garbage collector in the Finalizer makes the timing of the referencing to be uncertain. Below is an example.

```
public class Manager
{
    public Manager(string text)
    {
        System.Console.WriteLine(text);
    }
    ~Manager()
    {
        System.Console.WriteLine("FinalCommand!");
    }
    public static void Main()
```

```
    {
        ManagerMercy = new Manager("Created!");
        Mercy = null;
    }
}
```

The resultant output will be:

```
Created!
FinalCommand!
```

Properties

These are members of a class that define the functionality used in methods by application of syntax in fields. They present a simplified syntax of calls leading to traditional get-set methods.

They also share similarities with methods such as the existence of instance or static formats. They can be illustrated in the following format: (Let IntegerField is represented by IntField)

```
public class MyNumbers
{
    private int intField = 5; // Sets intField with a default value of 5
    public int IntField
    {
        get {
                return intField; // get- it returns the field you specify when this
        property is assigned.
        }
        set {
        intField = value; // set-it assigns the value assigned to the property of the
        field that was specified
                }
        }
}
```

13

Understanding the Property Code

The Keyword for declaring a property is value. Once a property is declared, it can be viewed as a variable. For instance, if some line of code could be added into the get-set part, the property would act as a method. This will enable the programmer to use the data before it is viewed as a variable. The example below shows how a property can be protectively used to ensure that data is secured and protected.

```
using System;
public class MyCoding
{
MyNumber mynumber = new MyNumber;
Console.WriteLine(myNumber.IntegerField); // Writes three(3) to the
command line.
myNumber.IntegerField = 9; // Indirectly assigns 9 to the field
myNumber.integerField
}
```

Indexer

These are members of a class that declare the operational behavior of an array access. The perfect example of this is list [0] for accessing the initial element in a list that is not in any array.

The keyword for defining an indexer is this. The example below shows how an indexer is created.

```
public string this[string key]
{
get {return coll[key];}
set {coll[key] = value;}
}
```

Understanding the Code

The code above will create the string indexer which will return the string value.

Events

These are members of a class that usually provide a notification to the clients that exist in a class.

Operators

These are members of a class that provides definition to the behavior of other C# basic operators on any instance of a specific class.

Structures

They are usually defined by a structs keyword that is accompanied by an identifier on the name of the structure. They share similarities with classes but with little differences.

They are used as lighter or summarized versions of the classes because they conserve memory when they work with minute data structures. Despite the fact that they conserve memory, they are least preferred as compared to standard classes.

There is a major difference between the structs and classes. The difference occurs in the instance of the two principles. The instance of the class is the references whereas the instance of the structs are values. For instance, when structs are passed via a function, a copy of the object is obtained hence the entire effect does not affect the original since there is a replica of the same. On the other end, when it is passed through a class, there is only a single instance.

The example below shows the declaration of a public and a private field. Accessing the private field is enabled through the public property "Naming":

```
struct Manager
{
  private string naming;
  public int YearOfBirth;
  public string Naming
  {
    set { naming = value; }
    get { return naming; }
  }
}
```

Static Classes

These types of classes are commonly used in the implementation of the **Singleton Pattern**. It is important to notice that all the properties are static and can be used without instantiation of static classes as shown below;

```
public static class Editor
{
  public static void Write()
  {
    System.Console.WriteLine("Word");
  }
}
public class Example
{
  public static void Main()
  {
    Editor.Write();
  }
}
```

Nested Classes

The C# language permits the existence of nested classes in which its defaults are returned to private. The program below is an example of a nested class.

```
class Code
{
    public class ClassInside
    {
        private int b;
    }
    static void Main(string[] args)
    {
    }
}
```

Inheritance and Interfacing of Classes

In C# programming language, the class is allowed to inherit either directly or indirectly from another base or basic class. This enables the implementation of multiple interfaces. It also entails an override of a defined method that is located in the base class. The keyword that is used for overriding is "override".

In addition, there is involvement of abstract and static classes. The keywords for defining the two classes are "abstract" and "static" respectively. The program below indicates an example of inheritance and interfacing of classes.

```
class theBasicClass{
public virtual void show(){
System.Console.WriteLine("basic class");}
}
interface Interface1{void showLecturer();}
```

```csharp
interface Interface2{void showStudent();}
class DeriveAndImplementeClass: BasicClass,Interface1,Interface2{
    public void showLecturer() { System.Console.WriteLine("Lecturer!");
}
    public void showStudent() { System.Console.WriteLine("Student!"); }
    public override void show(){
        System.Console.WriteLine("This is a derived Class");}
    static void Main(string[] args){
            DeriveAndImplementeClass de = new
DerivedAndImplementeClass();
            de.show();
            System.Console.Read();}
}
```

NOTE: *More details about the Advanced Operations in classes will be discussed in Chapter Two after the covering and understanding of the Dot Net Framework.*

Examples of simple C sharp program

In this area, we will utilize the examples to learn and examine different parts of the C# language. We will use this platform to comprehensively learn what has been applied. I would encourage the reader to be very careful and keen to learn from this example.

Example 1

```csharp
class HeyCSharp
{
  static void Main(string[] args)
  {
    System.Console.WriteLine("Hey C#!");
  }
}
```

18

Understanding our First Example

The program above prints the message "Hey C#" as the output. This is just a raw program that hasn't been compiled and run but can act as a good structure for learning our first C# programming language.

The program consists of three parts that are very logical. These are the;

- The Definition of the C# class **HeyCSharp**;

- The Definition of the C# method **Main()**;

- The Contents in the method **Main ()**.

The definition of the C# class

On the example, our first class in C# has been named as HeyCSharp. A class is identified by the Keyword "class" which is followed by the name of that class. The content of the class is surrounded by curly brackets.

The definition of the C# Method

This usually occurs on the third line and bears the initials **Main ()**. This is where our program begins followed a signature as shown below;

    static void Main(string[] args)

The method should always be declared as static and void as well as having the initials Main (). The list of parameters must have a parameter of one type which is of **type array of a string.** In our case we have used the "args" but it's not a must and can always be optional.

Note: *It is vital to notice that if the above requirements are violated, the program will not start since the compiler will not interpret it correctly.*

The Contents of the Method

These are the contents or anything that appears after the signature and are enclosed inside the curly brackets. In our example above, we used the System.Console and WriteLine() to output the message "HeyCSharp"

Example 2

The following example shows a typical structure of a C# language having the numbering before the coding. The learner should understand that the numbers are only significant for references purposes and they are not part of the program.

```
1. //Calculates and outputs the total traveling time
2. //for the traveling speed and covered distance
3. //Written by W M. Guru, 8/12/18
4.
5. using System;
6.
7. namespace InvitationCSharp
8. {
9.   class TravelOrganiser
10. {
11.   static void Main(string[] args)
12.   {
13.     int speed; //rate of over travel period
14.     Distance in both directions; //Kilometers to travel
15.     double time; //time required for the whole travel period
16.
17.     Console.Write("Input speed in kph: ");
```

```
18.     speed = Convert.ToInt32(Console.ReadLine());
19.     Console.Write("Input distance in kilometers: ");
20.     distance = Convert.ToDouble(Console.ReadLine());
21.
22.     time = distance / speed;
23.
24.     Console.Write("at " + speed + " mph, ");
25.     Console.WriteLine("you will take ");
26.     Console.Write(time + " hours to cover ");
27.     Console.WriteLine(distance + " kiloneters.");
28.     }
29.  }
30. }
```

The Output of the Code

Input your speed in mph: 48
Input your distance in Kilometers: 660
at 48 kph, you will take 13.75 hours to cover 660 kilometers.
Press any key to continue . . .

Understanding Our Example 2

The example above has introduced the numbering system which is used for reference. For instance, the lines 1-3 are C# commenting styles to give the learner the guidelines about the codes. The compiler ignores the execution of the comments because they are enclosed in the slash symbol.

The higher level languages have a way of guiding the human readers by the use of comments. This makes it for secondary human readers to understand the codes that have been written by a primary programmer. In summary, it is necessary to use comments because they act as headlines and guidelines to a written program.

In the above example we can also note some blank lines. The blank lines are used to make the written programs to be more readable and well-organized for proofreading. In the above program the blank lines include; 4, 6, 16, 21 and 23.

Line 5 utilizes a directive that makes a reference to the program's system library. The system library is equipped with such directives for reference purposes.

Line 7 shows the creation of a namespace for the coding. The namespaces are usually used in organizing the libraries in order to avoid ambiguous referencing of objects.

Line 9 shows a definition of a class hence exposing the header of the class. The name given to that class is TravelOrganiser. The lines 10 and 29 are curly braces that enclose the definition of the TravelOrganiser class.

Line 11 shows the main function. The main function is enclosed by curly braces in line 21 and 28.

Lines 13 to 15 are simply the declarations and the contents that are included in the Main function.

The rest of the lines 16-23, are codes, initials and system statements that are used in writing the program. They are commonly referred to as the heart of the program. They include statements such as Write, WriteLine, ReadLine, Console and others.

In summary, lines 24 to 27 show the output that will be displayed on the screen. This will interact with the user. Other important points to note in this example are that C# is free- formatting language. This means that the position of things in a line cannot affect the code but it is advised to be neat and smart in presenting your codes.

Example 3

The example below is meant for the learner to fish out some of the characteristics that have been taught above and to note the things that are missing. Please be keen on the example below.

```
using System;
namespace typical_trivial{
class House{
private int location;
protected string name;
public House(){
name = "No Name Yet!";
}
// every class inherits 'object' that has ToString()
public override string ToString(){
string disp = "Name is " + name + ", location= " +
location.ToString();
return disp;
}
}

class Program{
static void Main(string[] args){
House h = new House();
for (int i = 0; i < 4; i++){
System.Console.WriteLine("i={0}, house says:
{1}", i, h.ToString());
}
System.Console.Read();
}
}
}
```

23

1) What do you understand from the example above

2) What new features have you noted from the above example?

SUMMARY OF THE C# LANGUAGE

- C# Language is a modern, high-level language that is also a general purpose and object-oriented. Having been derived from C, it bears similar characteristics to both C and C++ programming languages. Despite the derivation, it is evident that it is an improved and simplified version of the two languages.

- The program is usually saved and has an extension of ".cs" before compilation. After the compiler has worked on the program, the executable codes are generated and appear with the extension ".exe" or ".dll".

- The some of the keywords that exist in the C# language include; **abstract, as, base, bool, break, byte, case, catch, char, checked, class, const, continue, decimal, default, delegate, do, double, else, enum, event, explicit, extern, false, finally, fixed, float, for, foreach, goto, if, implicit, in, int, interface ,internal, is, lock, long, namespace, new, null, among other keywords.**

- However, the C# language does not utilize all the available keywords.

– The main elements of a C# language consist of; ***classes, operators, conditional statements, methods, expressions, data types, loops, exceptions among other minor elements.***

Exercises

1. A written program will compute a value of 74 for the variable *length*. Generate an output statement that will display this variable using 12 columns, each on its own line.

2. What will appear on the display when the following statements have been executed?
   Console.Write("These is");
   Console.WriteLine("good morning");

3. Find, install and interact with Microsoft Visual Studio and Microsoft Developer Network (MSDN) Library Documentation.

4. Research about the "System.Console" class in the Dot Net API documentation (MSDN Library).

5. Research about the "System.Console.WriteLine()" method and the possible parameters that work with it in the MSDN Library.

6. Correct any sample program to display a different welcoming message, for example "Welcome Beloved!".

7. Create a console application that displays your surname and the first name on the console.

8. Write a code that displays the following integer numbers on the console 2, 201, 2001, each on its own line.

25

9. Write a code that displays on the console the current time.

10. Write a code that displays the square root of 625.

11. Write a code that displays the first 50 members of the sequence 3, - 4, 5, -6, 7, -8, 9.

12. Write a code that displays your friend's age from the console and prints the age after 5 years.

13. Distinguish the boundaries differentiating C# and the .NET Framework.

14. Create a list containing the most popular programming languages and how are they different from C#?

Points to Note.

❖ The C# language is case sensitive. It differentiates between lower case and upper case during the writing of the code. This points to the student that he or she should be careful on choosing the correct casing.

❖ The format of the program must be correct and accurate. Formatting entails operations like spacing, use of tabs, and addition of new lines among others. This contributes greatly to the logical structure of the C# language hence making the coding to be easy to use.

❖ The following are a short summary of the formatting rules.

i) The methods are moved towards the right by a single tab away from the definition of the classes.

ii) The contents of the method are moved towards the right (Indented) away from the definition of the mother method.

iii) The curly brackets must be on their own line. The opening and closing curly brackets should be on the same line vertically.

iv) All the class names and method names must begin with an upper case letter.

v) The variable names should start with a lower case letter.

❖ The code indentation follows a common rule that when a piece of codes lies inside another code, it should be moved towards the right by a single tab.

❖ The file names are preferred to correspond to the name of the original class. For example, if the name of the initial class is HeyCSharp, the file name should be HeyCsharp.cs. When these requirements are violated, the program will work but navigation of the codes will be very hectic.

Chapter Two

The Dot Net (.NET) Structure in C sharp language

Introduction

The Dot Net framework is an environment that allows the opportunity for programmers to build, run and deploy web applications and services as well as Window application. This platform consists of common libraries elements of a class such as ASP.NET, ADO.NET among others that are used to offer sufficient services that can be an integration of several computer systems.

This can also be defined as a tool used for development on the Windows and Web platforms. This is because it allows the computer developer/ programmer to freely access the external host system from the primary or any other computer. However, the Dot Net platform is only limited to the windows environment since other operating systems have their own defined platforms. Factors that affect such differences in platform include; interfaces, input/output management and security factors.

Background Information on the Dot Net platform

The platform was originally developed as NEXT GENERATION WINDOWS SERVICES (NGWS). It was based on the newest developing standards of the webs. The platform is restricted and cannot run on any random browser. The Dot Net was created and developed based on Internet Standards. The following are examples of Internet standards;

- UDDI-used for searching and discovering Web services.

- XML-used as a platform for the exchanging of data by Internet applications.

- HTTP-is a protocol used for communication by Internet applications.

- SOAP-Platform of request for Web services.

In addition, the following are languages that are integrated or use the Dot Net Platform;

- C# language

- A# language- ADA version

- J# language- Java version

- L# language-LISP Version

- Visual Basics

- Iron Ruby- Ruby Version

The Dot Net Technologies

The Dot Net is a big platform that is very comprehensive and complicated. However, it is not self-independent software that provides all solutions but works along with other independent technologies. Some of the recognized companies that work with this platform to provide sets of components include the Telerik and Bulgarian Software Companies.

The Dot Net extensions are components that can be used in the development of related programs. These components allow for reusable features of the codes which in turns makes software development to be a simple task. The advantages that come along with this feature are that common problems are solved, complex algorithms can be developed and solve multiple problems and a common technology can be advanced with a lot of ease. At the end of the day, a programmer can utilize the library components frequently hence saving a lot of effort.

There are a lot of Dot Net technologies that are spread out in developing software and web technologies. A good example of a web technology in the Dot Net Platform includes **ASP.NET** which enables a contemporary programmer to create dynamic web applications and services easily. On the other end, the Dot Net mobile technologies include; **WinJS.** This mobile technology allows the programmer to create a complex interface for multimedia applications on the internet.

In summary, the Dot Net technology is a compilation of Dot Net classes, tools, standards, libraries and programming models which determines the type of technology that will be used to create a particular type of application. Examples of such technologies include; **ADO.NET**

Developing console programs

Input

The gathering of the input and output are almost similar as will be seen later in the chapter. It uses the following methods; Read () and ReadLine (). Both methods come from the System.Console class. The example below shows a simple illustration.

```
using System;
public class SampleClass
{
public static void Main()
    {
Console.WriteLine("Hello! What is your first name?");
Console.Write("My first name is: ");
string name = Console.ReadLine();
Console.WriteLine("It was nice to know you, " + name);
Console.Read();// awaits the user's response to press any key before the
program exits.
    }
}
```

Understanding the Code

The program in the illustration above asks for the user's first name and outputs it in the display.

Output

Here, we are going to use an example in order to understand the concept of console programming. The following is an example of different ways to represent the output.

```
using System;
public class WelcomeToCSharpWorld
{
```

```
public static void Main()
    {
Console.WriteLine("Welcome to CSharp World!"); // depends on "using
System;"
Console.Write("I enjoy");
Console.Write("... learning this language!\n");
System.Console.WriteLine("It is very interesting!"); // no "using"
statement required
    }
}
```

The Resultant Output will be;

Welcome to CSharp World!
I enjoy... learning this language!
It is very interesting!

The text is displayed because of the use of the class of System.Console. The compiler is able to find the Console class since the "using" statement was used at the top of the program. The line at the middle uses the method Write () making it not to create another line. In order to create or maneuver to a new line, the sequence (\n) is used. In addition, the (\\n) is used to show the character. In the C# language, the backslash character is referred to as the escape character. It enables the programmer to encode other special characters.

Errors

The error output is mainly applicable in the diversion of specific console error messages. This may seem similar to the output above but it has a minor difference. It is applicable to the Console.Error stream. The Console.Error stream can be applied to the program in order to detect any type of error that occurs on the program coding. It is also used to monitor the probability of errors that may occur in the coding of a program and hence provide the feedback.

In the modern world, the Console.Error stream is modified so that they do not display the error message after every error but compile them into a log file. This advancement

Command line arguments

These are values that are scanned by the console program before they are executed. For instance, a copy command is included in a Windows command prompt before execution hence it's a combination of two line arguments. The initial argument contains the original file whereas the later argument contains the location for the new set or copy. Let's follow the illustration below;

```
using System;
public class SampleClass
{
public static void Main(string[] args)
    {
Console.WriteLine("Surname: " + args[0]);
Console.WriteLine("Middle Name: " + args[1]);
Console.Read();
    }
}
```

Explanation

If the above-illustrated program happens to be run on a compiler and saved as "usersname.exe", then it can be compiled or executed by a second argument for example "Brown" and "Wesley"

C:\>username.exe Brown Wesley

From the above program, we realize that the method contains a parameter of a string array. This means that the program expects more than a single argument. However, such like expectations make the safety of the program to be compromised. For instance, when the program is run without a proper definition of the number of line arguments then it will crash upon the missing line arguments. In order to overcome this weakness, the program is modified to know the expected number of line argument as shown below;

```
using System;
public class SampleTest
{
public static void Main(string[] args)
    {
if(args.Length >= 1)

Console.WriteLine(args[0]);// argument 1
if(args.Length >= 2)
Console.WriteLine(args[1]);// argument 2
    }
}
```

Explanation

When a user tries to run the program by inputting a single name or empty name, the string.Length characteristic will return the collectively total number of line arguments.

NOTE: *The programmer is able to group or gather one argument collectively by use of the"" quote symbols. This is useful in cases where there are multiple parameters and a requirement for inclusive spaces for example the file names and locations. Below is an illustration of the same.*

```
using System;
class SampleTest
{
public static void Main(string[] args)
   {
for(int index =0 ;index < args.Length; index++)
      {
Console.WriteLine((index+1) + ": " + args[index]);
      }
   }
}
```

C:\> Test.exe Separate words "Combined together"
1: Different
2: words
3: combined together

Windows Forms

This majorly discusses Graphical User Interface programming associated with Window Forms. It utilizes the namespace "System.Windows.Forms" that enables the creation of Window application in an easy manner.

In the achievement of this there is involvement of the Form Class which forms the basis of building blocks of all the Window applications. In the actual sense, the platform is created where the visual frame houses the icons, hold buttons, menus, title bars among other tools. On the other end, there are easier methods for creating graphical applications such as using IDEs like SharpDevelop and Visual C# .Despite other easier methods and procedures of creating a graphical application it is necessary to know the manual procedure as shown below.

```csharp
using System.Windows.Forms;
public class FormExample : Form // Does the inheritance  from
System.Windows.Forms.Form
{
    public static void Main()
    {
        FormExample weeklybooksForm = new FormExample();
        weeklybooksForm.Text = "I Read Weeklybooks";// specifying
the form title
        weeklybooksForm.Width = 500; // This entails the width of the
window( In Pixels)
        weeklybooksForm.Height = 400; //This entails the height (in
pixels)
        Application.Run(weeklybooksForm); // the action done here is
displaying the form
    }
}
```

Understanding our Program

When the codes above are run, they will create a (simple) Window that has a title bar that is written "I Read Weeklybooks". As shown above the Custom Form (Class) inherits directly from the System.Windows.Forms.

From the example above, we can notice the settings of the height and width. This is an optional characteristic that can be adapted by the programmer or be left out. The programmer is reminded to be careful in quoting the comments line so that the codes can be run and compiled successfully. The comment lines allow for the addition of controls in the new form.

Advanced Operations

In this section, we are going to revisit some advanced operations in more details and discuss them in a topical manner. We are going to learn these advanced features in a simpler way that will make you understand without straining. Some of the operations that we are going to discuss in this subtopic include the;

- Inheritance
- Interfaces
- Abstract classes
- Partial classes
- Object Lifetime

We are going to begin with;

Inheritance

This is defined as the ability to create or derive a new class from an existing class. In simple terms, other people prefer to liken it to a parent class generating a child or derived class. In the C# programming language, this ability of derivation can be accompanied by overloading property from the mother or parent class.

Inheritance keywords

These are the keywords that the C# language implements so that it can inherit from another class. Firstly it uses the ":" character as shown below;

```
public virtual void Write(string text)
{
System.Console.WriteLine("Text:{0}", text);
}
```

Secondly, we have to override a method. The keyword for overriding a method is "override" just as shown below;

```
public override void Write(string text)
{
System.Console.WriteLine(text);
}
```

In the example below, we are going to create a parent class so that we can derive a child class from it. In the parent class below are two classes, Manager and Director. The Manager class has two methods namely GetPayRoll and DailyDuty. Our objective is to ensure the Director class has similar methods despite being implemented differently with the addition of an extra method called NewManagerTask.

Below is the illustration of the above-explained classes;

A. Creation of the Parent class

In order to achieve this creation we have to mark a method with virtual so that it can be overridden.

```
public class Manager
{
// Here we declare a method virtual so that the Director class is able to
override it.
public virtual void GetPayRoll()
{
//acquire the payroll logic.
}
//Manager's and Director both have a daily duty, so they do not need a
virtual
public void DailyDuty()
{
```

```
//perform the work logic at this point.
}
}
```

B. Creation of the Child class

In order to create this class, we will create the Director class that will be overriding the GetPayRoll method.

```
public Manager : Director
{
// the override keyword indicates we want new logic behind the
GetPayRoll method.
public override void GetPayRoll()
{
//new getpayroll logic here.
}
// the extra method is implemented.
public void NewManagerTask()
{
// manage Managers logic here
}
}
```

Understanding our code

In the above code, the Manager class lacks the DailyDuty method. This is because it is not necessary since it was originally in the Manager class hence it does not need any other derivation from the Director class which contains the DailyDuty method.

C. Outcomes from the derivations

```
static void Main(string[] args)
{
Manager emp = new Manager;
```

```
Director exec = new Director;
emp.DailyDuty();
exec.DailyDuty();
emp.GetPayRoll();
exec.GetPayRoll();
exec.NewManagerTask();
}
```

Interfacing

An interface as used in C# language is a definition type feature that shares similarity with a class but independently represents a relationship between an object and its user. It is important to note that at this point the interface cannot be instantiated similar to an object. The example below shows an illustration;

```
interface IShape
{
void Draw();
double X { get; set; }
double Y { get; set; }
}
```

Note: *There is no definition of data member in an interface. In addition, the methods and properties should be declared and not to be defined.*

Understanding our Code1

In the Dot Net framework, an "I" is usually placed at the beginning of the naming of the interface in order to help the C# programmer to differentiate it easily from the name of the class. Secondly, the naming criteria are applicable when the interface performs a declaration of a single key method like the Draw () in the above illustration. For this

40

case, the suffix "able" is added to the method name so that in the example it would be ***IDrawable***. The procedure described above is applicable to the whole framework of the Dot Net platform

The implementation of the interface is achieved by complete-shift inheritance and definition of methods and properties which have been declared directly by the interface as shown below;

```
class Square : IShape
{
private double mY, mZ;

public void Draw() { ... }
public double Y
{
set { mY = value; }
get { return mY; }
}
public double Z
{
set { mZ = value; }
get { return mZ; }
}
}
```

Understanding Code 2

Despite the fact that classes only inherit from other classes, the inheritance of classes from an inheritance is also possible. A class can directly inherit from several numbers of existing interfaces. For this case, the base class is supposed to be in existences at the Inheritance list which should be followed by the interfaces that are supposed to be implemented as shown below;

```
class MyClass : Class1, Interface1, Interface2 { ... }
```

In summary, interfaces can perform inheritance from other interfaces but cannot obtain from the classes as illustrated below;

```
interface IRotateable
{
void Rotate(double theta);
}

Or

interface IDrawable : IRotateable
{
void Draw();
}
```

Point to Note about Interfacing

Interface members are not allowed to use the Access specifiers such as private, internal and others. This is because the entire members are actively public. The implementation of interfaces from classes must ensure a proper definition of the member as well as the declaration of the interface as public.

In addition, interfaces are able to declare the events and indexers that are found in methods and properties.

Abstract Classes

In C# programming language, there are a lot of relations from one component to the other. For instance, the C# interface can be defined as a set having public members. Likewise, the C# class can be defined as a set of interfaces. This is because it contains a set having public members.

Definition of an Abstract class

In C# programming language, it is absolutely possible to have an existing intermediate between an interface without any role or defined implementation and the type of interface that has a role or defined implementation. This is the definition of an **Abstract Class.**

The keyword that defines the abstract class is the **"abstract".** In simple terms, an abstract class can be defined as an intermediate of a C# interface and a Non-Abstract class. The example below is a perfect example of an abstract class that has a defined implementation from none of its belonging members.

```
public abstract class AnAbstractShape
{
public abstract void Draw(Graphics h);
public abstract double Y {get; set;}
public abstract double Z {get; set;}
}
```

The above class shows many similarities with the interface despite that the class above is able to derive from only that class but not from any other class. It is important to also recognize the fact that an abstract class can define all the existing members in that class just as shown below;

```
public abstract class AnAbstractShape
{
private double y;
private double z;
//
// ... (includes the other members)
//
public void Draw(Graphics g) {g.DrawSquare(Pencil.white, g_sqre);}
```

```
public double Y {get{return y;}}
public double Z {get{return z;}}
}
```

Alternatively, the abstract class is also able to define some of its members partially and leave other members undefined just as shown below;

```
public abstract class AnAbstractShape
{
private double y;
private double z;
//
// ... (includes the other members)
//
public abstract void Draw(Graphics h);
public double Y {get{return y;}}
public double Z {get{return z;}}
}
```

Points to note about Abstract classes

In this part we are going to differentiate and distinguish important contents and concepts about abstract and Non-abstract classes.

i) In the first instance, the abstract class cannot be instantiated with the **"new"** keyword. If this concept is violated, the compiler will raise an error.

ii) Abstract classes can contain abstract members. The Non-Abstract classes cannot have abstract members. On special occasions, when it is a must that the Non-Abstract classes contain an abstract member; the **"abstract"** keyword must be used.

iii) Sealing cannot be done with the Abstract classes. For instance, it is not possible to apply the two keywords ("abstract" and "sealed") in the same abstract class.

Partial classes

Just from the naming, it means partial classes can be defined from splitting of many physical files. The splitting does not affect the operation of the compiler since it is able to group the fragments of work as a single group. The compiler combines the fragments and runs them together as a simple component. The main and common application of partial classes is during the separation of programmer's written codes from the computer's generated codings.

Below is a good example of the creation of a partial class from an entire class which will make us understand further concepts.

A. The whole class

```
public class ANode
{
public bool Remove()
{}
public bool Add()
{}
}
```

B. Splitting of classes.

i. Split 1 (Splitfile1.cs)

```
public partial class ANode
{
public bool Remove()
```

```
{}
}
```

ii.   *Split 2 (Splitfile2.cs)*

```
public partial class ANode
{
public bool Add()
{}
}
```

In summary, the partial classes are used in C# programming language to make the programmer's code and the computer's code to be very distinctive. This can be helpful in the identification and correction of errors that may exist in the codes.

Object Lifetime

This topic is highly important to the learner in this programming language since this is the general concept that is used in the utilization and conservation of computer memory. From simple concepts, we know and understand that all computer programs and application require adequate memory space in order to run efficiently.

We are going to discuss the garbage collection feature in Dot Net Framework and C# programming language and how it manages the memory resources.

In some occasions, the learner can ask himself or herself about the concept behind the runtime environment management of memory during operation. The following are possible answers to your questions on how memory can be reclaimed by the runtime environment especially when it is not in use;

a) For the managed resources, the garbage collector automatically releases the memory.

b) For the unmanaged resources, an interface IDisposable is used to clean up and release the memory.

c) For a special case when the garbage collector is called directly, it is forced to clean up and release of memory immediately. This is accomplished by the use of System.GC.Collect () method.

The Garbage Collector

This can be defined as a background process that is always running within the program. It is important to know that this is a new feature that runs all the Dot Net Applications and its main role is conservation of memory.

This background process works by identification and cleanup of the objects that are not being used by the running program. For instance, when the object in the running program is assigned to zero or null, the garbage collector marks the objects and cleans up the object and hence releases its resources later.

The garbage collector always runs when there are limited resources. This is because some programs that require speed of operation have millions of zero assigned objects that are left "idle" but are very efficient in their running. The collector cannot always run in multiple Dot Net application to de-allocate objects and yet the resources are adequate.

From the above explanation and operations, we can now establish the reasons why the garbage collection operate in three regions listed below;

- **Generation 0**- deals with objects that have been created most recently

- **Generation 1**- deals with mid-life objects in the program

- **Generation 2**- deals with the objects that are long term.

In the above-mentioned generations, all the references of the objects must pass through those generations. The generations basically work in accordance with the lifetime of the object in the program. In summary, the garbage collector operates by removing what is not needed. On the other end, we need to know the types of resources that are managed by the garbage collector.

The types of resources managed by the garbage collector include;

    i) Managed resources.

    ii) Unmanaged resources.

Managed Resources

Managed Resources are those objects that run wholly and completely within the Dot Net framework. Just as mentioned before, the memories are completely reclaimed for the programmer since all the resources are closed down. The programmer is guaranteed to utilize all the memory when the garbage collector runs or when the application is closed. This whole process is automatic and occurs all by itself hence it is called "**self-tidying object**".

Unmanaged Resources

There are possibilities and circumstances when the Dot Net framework is not able to clean up or release the resources. This might occur most especially when the object references have been the source from somewhere outside the Dot Net framework. It can be sourced from the operating system or other unmanaged location or uses sources from COM or DCOM.

For instance, if the programmer is using any object that uses the IDisposable interfacing at any class level then the IDisposable interfaces have to be Re-implemented as shown below;

```
public interface IDisposable
{
public void Dispose();
}
```

Understanding our code

The method that is shown above shows the method that is called "Dispose ()". Since the above is only an interface, it cannot clean up or tidy up any resources. Because of this inability the programmer or developer must do the following steps in order to release the resources;

a. The developer must call the Dispose () method frequently on an object so that it implements the interface IDisposable every time the programmer is done with the program. For easier steps, the developer is advised to use the appropriate keyword.

b. The developer should utilize the Finalizer method on a frequent basis to call the Dispose () method so that if any closure has not been done on the resources then the code will automatically do it itself.

From this subtopic we are able to finalize and justify the reason why the C# programming language is the advanced version of the C programming language. I hope you harvested a lot of knowledge from this chapter. We have established the background knowledge of the basic things about C# programming language.

Let's get to learn more in the next chapter.

Chapter Three

Existence of various Data Types, Constants and Variables in C sharp Programming Language

Data types

What are Data types?

Data types can be defined as a range (set) of values that have similar features and characteristics. In some other cases, data values have similar characteristics that do define them and hence it is very necessary to learn some of the features while we use C# programming language.

These are features that make the programmer group data in classes and they include the following;

- *Name*
- *Default value*
- *Size*

The basic data types that exist in the C# programming language do exist in various types. They are usually referred to as **Primitive data types.** This is because they are built in the C# language even up to the lowest level. The types of Basic data types include;

- **Object type**- object

- **Character type**- char

- **Boolean type**-bool

- **String type**- string

- **Real type (having decimal precision)**- decimal

- **Real types (float-pointing)** - double, float.

- **Integer type**- ulong, long, ushort, short, byte, sbyte, uint, int.

The table below shows an example of the above-listed data types having their ranges and default values.

Example of data types	Maximum values	Minimum Values	Default Values
short	32767	-32768	0
ushort	65535	0	0
long	9223372036854775807	-9223372036854775808	0L
ulong	18446744073709551615	0	0u
int	2147483647	-2147483648	0
uint	4294967295	0	0u
byte	255	0	0
sbyte	127	-128	0
string	-	-	null
double	$\pm1.7\times10^{308}$	$\pm7.9\times10^{28}$	0.0d
decimal	$\pm7.9\times10^{28}$	$\pm1.0\times10^{-28}$	0.0
object	-	-	null
char	'\uffff'	'\u0000'	'\u0000'
float	$\pm3.4\times10^{38}$	$\pm1.5\times10^{-45}$	0.0
bool	True or false	True or false	false

In summary, the built-in data types which are also called primitive data types are directly connected with the common types (CTS) that exist in the Dot Net Framework. The existence of these common types system (CTS) in the Dot Net framework makes programming languages to be very compatible with each other. Examples of programming languages that are compatible with each other because of this feature include; C#, F#, C++ and VB.NET.

We are going to briefly discuss the data types so that we can be very conversant with the data types that we will encounter during our programming sessions.

Integer types

The integer types include numbers and examples that have been listed and we shall pass through each one of them so that we can have a better understanding.

a) Short- this is a signed integer that has 16 bits.

b) Ushort- this is the unsigned version of integers that also has 16 bits.

c) Long- this is a signed integer that has 64 bits.

d) Ulong- this is the unsigned version of the integers that have 64 bits. It is important to note that this is the biggest type of integer.

e) Int- this is a signed integer that has 32 bits. This type of integer happens to be commonly used in most types of programming languages. It is naturally used in 32-bit computers and microprocessors for daily calculations.

f) Uint-this is the unsigned version of the 32-bit integers.

g) Byte- this is the unsigned version of the 8 bits integers

h) Sbyte- this type is the signed integers that have 8 bits.

Now that we know the types of integers we are dealing with, it is important that we have an example of codings and get to understand the code afterwards.

```
// Declaration of some of the variables
byte centuries = 10;
ushort years = 1000;
uint days = 365240;
ulong hours = 8765760;
// here the result of the console is printed
Console.WriteLine(centuries  + " centuries have " + years +
" years, or " + days + " days, or " + hours + " hours.");
// here the output of console is displayed:
// 10 centuries have 1000 years, or 365240 days, or 8765760
// hours.
ulong maxIntValue = UInt64.MaxValue;
Console.WriteLine(maxIntValue); // 18446744073709551615
```

Understanding our code

In the example above, several variables have been declared, initialized and printed out to the console. The codings above have shown a little demonstration of the use of some integer types. For example, unsigned integer data types have been used for values that have positive numbers. In addition, the ulong data types are used for large numbers whereas the byte data type is used for small values.

Real types (float-pointing)

These are common types of real numbers that are used in common mathematical calculations. As mentioned before, the float-pointing real types are represented by double and float.

a) **Float**- it is also referred to as single precision. At the default value, the 'f' used as an allocation of the name float. It has an accuracy level up to the seventh decimal for example; 0.12345678 will be rounded off to 0.1234568.

b) **Double**- it is also referred to as double precision. At the default value, the 'd' is used to indicate such. The precision in this type can go up to 16 decimal numbers. In addition, this type of precision can take in the special values for example; double.positive infinity, invalid numbers and double.negative infinity.

Note: the real types have special values which are mathematically abstract but they are not real numbers as listed below;

- **Negative infinity**- this is obtained during the division of default numbers such as 0.0f and -1.0f

- **Uncertainity**- it is obtained by performing an invalid calculation using real numbers for example the square root of negative numbers.

- **Positive Infinity**- this result is obtained during operation of the division of 1.0f and 0.0f

Real type (Having decimal precision)

C# programming language allows numbers to be represented using the decimal number system as compared to other languages that use the binary number system. It has a decimal precision ranging from 28 to 29 decimal placing. At the default value, the 'm' indicates that the type is a real number with decimal precision.

This type of precision is very accurate during calculations and storage. It is important to note that the major difference between floating-point and decimal precision real data type is the accuracy and storage bit and criterion. Because of the high level of accuracy, it is widely used in financial institutions for complex calculation and storage of data.

Boolean type

This is declared by the word "**bool**". It works on the basis of two options; either true or false. In most of the cases, the default value of the Boolean type is false. The following is an example of declaration and initialized codes.

```
// Declaration of some of the variables

int a = 10;
int b = 20;
// Which of the two greater?
bool greaterAB = (a > b);
// Is 'a' equal to 10?
bool equalA1 = (a == 10);
// Printing of the results in the console
if (greaterAB)
{
Console.WriteLine("A > B");
}
else
```

```
{
Console.WriteLine("A <= B");
}
Console.WriteLine("greaterAB = " + greaterAB);
Console.WriteLine("equalA1 = " + equalA1);
// Console output is displayed:
// A <= B
// greaterAB = False
// equalA1 = True
```

Character type

It consists of a 16-bit single character. It is declared by the keyword "char". The numbers of this type are represented using a UNICODE TABLE. The smallest recognizable character is the 0 and the highest is 65535. The values of this type are usually enclosed in apostrophes wherever they are used.

The following is an example of a program that has an application of character type.

```
// Declaration of a variable
char ch = 'b';
// Print the results on the console
Console.WriteLine(
"Our coding of '" + ch + "' should be: " + (int)ch);
ch = 'c';
Console.WriteLine(
"Our coding of '" + ch + "' should be: " + (int)ch);
ch = 'D';
Console.WriteLine(
"Our coding of '" + ch + "should be: " + (int)ch);
// Console output is displayed:
// Our coding of 'b' should be: 98
```

57

```
// Our coding of 'c' should be: 99
// Our coding of 'D' should be: 66
```

String type

A string can be simply defined as a sequence of known characters. They are declared by the keyword "**string**". The default value of the string type is usually null. They are usually enclosed using quotation marks. They are commonly used in text processing such as replacing characters, conducting searches and concatenation.

The following is a program that uses string type, I hope we are going to observe the usage of string type from it.

```
// Declaration of some of the variables
string firstName = "James";
string lastName = "Smokin";
string fullName = firstName + " " + lastName;
// Display the results on the console
Console.WriteLine("Hey, " + firstName + "!");
Console.WriteLine("Your two names are " + fullName + ".");
// Console output:
// Hey, James!
// your two names are James Smokin.
```

Object type

This is a special type that exists in the Dot Net framework. It is usually declared by the keyword "object". The special type takes literally any value from any other data type.

The following is an example of a program that utilizes object type.

```
// Declaration of some of the variables
object bucket1 = 4;
object bucket2 = "Four";
```

// **Display the results on the console**
Console.WriteLine("The kilograms of bucket1 is: " + bucket1);
Console.WriteLine("The kilograms of bucket2 is: " + bucket2);
// Console output:
// The kilograms of container1 is: 4
// The kilograms of container2 is: Four.

Nullable Data Types

These are specific data types that are usually referred to **as wrappers**. They are used to store data that contain null values. This is basically an allowance to those types of data that lack values. They can freely be used for referencing and can now be accepted as either normal or special values. At other times, the nullable data types hold the **optional data values.**

Wrapping of data values can be achieved in two major ways;

Nullable<int> i1 = null; // the first way (complex)
int? i2 = i1; // the second way (easiest)

The declarations that have been done above are both equivalent to each other. The best way to conduct this declaration is the addition of the question mark.

In summary, the nullable data type can also be referred to as reference data types. This is because they usually contain the actual values that are stored in the dynamic memory and hence they are referred to by the objects. The following is an example of codes bearing nullable data types;

int i = 4;
int? ni = i;
Console.WriteLine(ni); // 4

```
// i = ni; // this shall not compile
Console.WriteLine(ni.HasValue); // this is True
i = ni.Value;
Console.WriteLine(i); // 4
ni = null;
Console.WriteLine(ni.HasValue); // this is False
//i = ni.Value; // System.InvalidOperationException
i = ni.GetValueOrDefault();
Console.WriteLine(i); // 0
```

Understanding our code;

From the example above, it shows the declaration of the null data type by the use of a question mark (int?). This means that a value can be added freely whether the value is nullable or non-nullable. The default value for the nullable data type is zero (0).

These data types are used in the storage of information. The type of information stored by this data type is the less important and less mandatory data.

Variables

A variable can be described as a store of information. On the other end, variables can be used in retrieval, modification and processing of stored data. The example below is a simple illustration;

```
string name = "Mrs. Evelyn";
Console.WriteLine("Hello Good Afternoon " + name);
```

Understanding the example

In the above example, the name is the identifier while "Mrs. Evelyn" is a value assigned to the identifier. It is important to note that values whose data types that are only compatible with the variable are the ones that are being stored.

Characteristics of Variables

In C# programming language, the variables can be characterized and identified by the following features;

- Name- this is the identifier.

- Type- this is the reserved information in the variable for example; **int;**

- Value- this is the stored information in the variable.

Variables are used to store values of a specific data type. Variables can either be stored in the dynamic memory or the stack memory. This depends on the type of data and also the size of the data to be stored by the variable.

The primitive data types such as bool, and char store their data values in the stack whereas the reference data types store their data values in the dynamic memory. This is because the primitive data types are smaller in size than the reference data types hence can be stored in the stack. On the other end, the reference type such as strings, arrays and objects are stored in the dynamic memory and can be accessed directly.

Elements of Variables in C# Programming Language

The C# programming language contains elements that support the whole programming concept pertaining to variables such as *fields, local variables and parameters.*

Fields

These are variables that are mostly associated with structures and classes. They can also be referred to as "**Class-level Variables**". In the fields are instance and static variables. An Instance variable refers to the fields that are directly associated with the instance of a structure or class. A static variable is a field that is independent and associated with it. It is usually declared by the keyword "**static**".

The fields can either be private, public, protected, and internal or protected internal.

Local variables

The local variables share some similarities with fields. Some of the similarities include being an optionally a constant. The constant variables (local) are usually stored in the assembly or central data region whereas the non-constant variable is stored in the stack.

Parameters

Parameters can be defined as variables that are generally associated with methods. There are several types of parameters. We are going to briefly describe the types in a simple way so that we can understand their working principles.

The *in-parameter-* its values can either have passed by the callee all the way to the method. In this case, the changes that are made to the parameter do not affect those in the callee.

The *out-parameter-* its values are neither passed through the method environment hence the changes that are made are affected to the parameter. Both the callee's and method environment affect each other during slight changes.

The *reference-parameter-* it shares the most similarities with the *out-parameter*. The major difference reflects when it is bound immediately before the method call. This type of parameter is not bound to be assigned to any method.

The *params-parameter-* this type of parameter represents a number of other parameters. The example below shows a sample of explanation of the parameters;

// Each pair of lines is the definition of a method. A call of each method with each of the parameter types would look like.

In param:
void MethodOne(int param1)
MethodOne(variable); //call
// Out param:
void MethodTwo(out string message)
MethodTwo(out variable); //call
// the Reference param;
void MethodThree(ref int someFlag) //definition
MethodThree(ref theFlag) //call
// Params
void MethodFour(params string[] names) //definition
MethodFour("Genesis", "Exodus", "Leviticus", "Number"); //call

Naming of variables

Naming operations are necessary for identification and references operations. For instance, the compiler must find a name for a storage location of data values. For this case, there are restrictions that relate to the naming of variables specifically confined in C# programming language as listed below;

- They can contain the alphabetical letters both in uppercase (A-Z) or lower case (a-z) and numbers (0-9).

- A variable name cannot start with a number for example; 9XXXX

- A variable name is allowed to have this character "_".

- A variable name cannot be the same as a Keyword in C# programming language.

NOTE: *the names of the variables should be clear, precise and descriptive to its purpose or its use.*

Declaration of Variables

Declaration of variables is done in three steps;

i) Specification of the type for example **int;**

ii) Specification of the name which is the identifier.

iii) Specification of initial values

The basic structure (syntax) of declaration of data type is;

<data type> <identifier> [= <initialization>];

For example;

string name;
int YearOfBirth;

Assigning of Values

This is the process of providing values that should be stored by the variable. The process is made a success by the operator "=". The example below shows the assigning of values to the variables using an assignment operator.

Example 1

```
name = "James";
YearOfBirth = 1975;
```

Example 2

```
// Declaration and initialization of some the variables
byte centuries = 10;
ushort years = 1000;
decimal decimalPI = 3.141592653589793238m;
bool isEmpty = true;
char ch = 'b';

string firstName = "James";
ch = (char)4;
char secondChar;
// Here reassigning and usage of the initialized variable is done.
secondChar = ch;
```

Summary

Generally, the data types that exist in C# programming language can be classified as either reference or value.

Reference types are stored in the dynamic memory. They also perform allocation of the dynamic memory for their own use. They contain references and addresses of operation of data where the values are stored. The reference acts as a pointer to the dynamic memory commonly referred to as a heap hence shows the actual location of the heap. All the references can hold a nullable data type referred to as a special character. The reference types also perform functions such as memory cleaning using the principle of the garbage collector as studied before. The reference types include arrays, classes and interfaces. The examples include; string, object and byte. In summary, the data types that have no values are reference data types and are stored in the dynamic memory or heap memory.

On the other end, the value types are usually stored in the program stack. They are stored directly after execution to the place that has the relative value. The value type consists of the following; primitive data types, the Boolean type and the character type. It is important to note that, the memory allocated for this data type is released when the program closes its use. Examples of the value type include; *bool, char, long, short, int, float, decimal, double, byte, ulong, ushort and sbyte.*

Chapter Four

Data Structures, Handling and Functions

Introduction and Significance of Data Structures

In this chapter we are going to learn about the definition of data structures and their significance in the C# programming language. We will learn on the importance of the data structures and when and how to use them during the programming sessions. It is equally important to know that a great programmer writes efficient and effective programs using very appropriate data structures.

Programming is made up of two major components. These are algorithms and data structures. This explains the reason why more attention is given to these two components. A good developer or software engineer is that which has vast skills and knowledge of data structures and efficient in programming.

Before we get deeper into the data structure there are few terms that we should know and understand in order to become a good developer. **Algorithm complexity-**this can be defined as a standard which examines the order of the operations count that is performed and evaluated by an algorithm which becomes a function of input data size. This standard is commonly represented by **O (f) notation** which is referred to as **"Big O notation or asymptotic notation".** There are many types of complexities such as constant, logarithmic, exponential, linear, cubic and, quadratic.

Enumerations, Arrays and structs

Enumerations

This can be defined as a data type that specifies the number of items by equally assigning them to an identifier for example a name. This is made possible by the consideration of the underlying pattern of the base type of the components of the specification or the enumeration.

The declaration of an enumeration can be done as shown below;

enum Months { January, February, March, April, May, June, July, August, September, October, November, December };

Understanding our code

The code above portray elements of enumerations which are displayed as constants as shown below;

```
Month = Month.January;
if (month == Month.February)
{
Console.WriteLine("Programming with C# through the months of the
year is easy!");
}
```

The first element is always a zero when there is no explicit value which is assigned to the specified or enumerated items. The subsequent elements will uptake the successive value after zero. On the other end, the specific values that originate from integral types can always be assigned to specified elements of enumeration as shown below;

```
enum Age { Baby = 0, Adolescence = 13, Youth = 18 };
Age age = Age.Adolescence
```

Console.WriteLine("You are an adolescence at the age of {0}.",
(int)age);

In addition, values that are underlying in the specified elements of enumeration usually go unused when the grouping function is specific to a certain group of data. It is usually advisable to create a specified element list using base type as compared to int.

Arrays

This is a representation of a group of items of a similar type or those that bear similar characteristics. The declaration of arrays may depend on constants and variables. It is important to note that once the array length has been declared it cannot be altered after declaration as shown below;

```
// an array whose length is defined with a constant
int[] integers = new int[10];
int length = 0;
System.Console.Write("what is the length of an array? ");
System.Console.ReadLine(length);
// this is an array. Its length has been defined with a variable

// Arrays do not change their length after declaration
double[] doubles = new double[length];
```

Structs

The keyword that is used to declare a struct is "**struct**". They are referred to as light container weight for objects. They are mostly applied when data is needed for collection of types of variables.

Structs can be compared to classes. Structs have methods, constructors and interfaces. The other major differences include;

- Structs are usually the value types whereas the classes are considered to be reference types.

- Structs cannot inherit as compared to classes.

- Structs require a less memory space and is less expensive as compared to classes.

- Structs have a compulsory default constructor even if it is not required whereas a class gives the allowance to hide the constructors.

Declaration of structs is done as follows;

```
struct Girl
{
public string name;
public System.DateTime birthDate;
public int heightInMtrs;
public int weightInGrams;
}
```

The Person Struct is used as follows;

```
Girl dana = new Girl();
dana.name = "Dana Programmer";
dana.birthDate = new DateTime(1975, 8, 19);
dana.heightInMtrs = 1.75;
dana.weightInGrams = 50000;
if (dana.birthDate < DateTime.Now)
{
Console.WriteLine("Dana Programmer is a genuine programmer!");
}
```

The example below shows how constructors can be used in structs for initialization;

```
using System;
struct Girl
{

string name;
DateTime birthDate;
int heightInMtrs;
int weightInGrams;
public Person(string name, DateTime birthDate, int heightInMtrs, int
weightInGrams)
{
this.name = name;
this.birthDate = birthDate;
this.heightInMtrs = heightInMtrs;
this.weightInGrams = weightInGrams;
}
}
public class StructWeeklyBookSample
{
public static void Main()
{
Person dana = new Person("Dana Programmer", new DateTime(1975, 8,
19),
1.75, 50000);
}
}
```

In summary, structs are best used for performance reasons. They work best when they are holding data amounting to 16bytes but if the programmer is in doubt he or she can utilize the classes.

Relationship between Data Structures Using Algorithm Complexities

At this point we are going to study and compare the different data structures using algorithm complexities. We are going to encounter with operations such as searching, addition, deletion and accessing of data by use of indexing. This will also help us in choosing which data structure to use when programming or developing our codes. The table below is an illustration of basic operations done by the complexities;

Data structure	Search	Addition	Deletion	Index Access
Array	O(N)	O(N)	O(N)	O(1)
Dynamic array	O(N)	O(1)	O(N)	O(1)
Linked lists	O(N)	O(1)	O(N)	0(N)
Stack	-	O(1)	O(1)	-
Queue	-	O(1)	O(1)	-
Balance search tree (set)	O(log(N))	O(log(N))	O(log(N))	-
Hash table (set)	O(1)	O(1)	0(1)	-
Balance search tree (Dictionary)	O(log(N))	O(log(N))	O(log(N))	-
Hash table(dictionary)	O(1)	O(1)	O(1)	-

When to choose a data structure

In this section of the book we are going to discuss situations in which the data structures listed in the table above is going to be used.

Array

As discussed before, this is a grouping or collection of number of components of a similar type. We can also refer to the arrays as "*a small container of data having a predefined size*". **Addition** of new elements into an array as shown in the table is a very slow process. For this to occur successfully, allocation of definite space is done and an extra space that can transfer data from one array to another. **Searching** of an array is also a slow process because the comparison is done in accordance to the needed value. **Deletion** of an element from the array is a slow process because it's a reverse of the addition process. In this case a definite memory is allocated and a single space is subtracted. However, accessing an array is very fast and efficient because it utilizes **indexing.**

Arrays are best for situations like processing fixed amount or number of components which should be accessed by the use of an index.

Dynamic Arrays

This is the most commonly used type of data structure in modern programming. This is because it avoids a fixed list of components and enables direct access of data by the use of indices. Dynamic arrays can also be referred to as an "array or resizable list".

Dynamic arrays usually hold elements in a list of array. The advantage of this array is that the list has a bigger size than the number of stored components. **Addition** into the dynamic array takes a specific constant time. This is because there is always an empty cell before the addition of components. **Searching** the dynamic array is a slow operation because there is traversing through all the stored components in order to find what is being looked for. **Deletion** from the dynamic array is a slow process. The execution of this command is done using linear time. The other reason is that once a deletion is made, the stored elements are moved to the left in order to create an empty cell for addition.

The dynamic array is used in situations that require quick addition and access by the use of indexing.

Linked lists

These can either be singly or doubly linked lists. The major function done by both the singly and doubly linked list is the storage of collection of components by maintaining their order. They are represented in the memory as dynamic and pointer-based.

Addition into the linked list is a very fast process. Although it is slower than dynamic arrays, it is an advanced process. This is achieved by a new allocation of memory space. It is a high-speed process that is always unpredictable. **Searching** is a very slow process because it uses the same principle as dynamic arrays to traverse all the elements during the search. **Deletion** of an element is a slow operation. This is because searching is done before deletion hence the indexing process makes it generally slow.

In summary, a linked list has a fast addition process. It is suitable for situations when addition and removal are needed at a faster rate at both sides of the linked lists.

Stack

This is a linear data structure that has three major steps; addition of components to the top of the specific stack(push), removing components from the top of the specific stack(pop) and inspection of the components at the top of the stack without interfering with the order(peek).

The **addition and deletion** of the stack is a very fast process because a constant time is used. The stack does not have the searching and accessing by index features. It generally works with the LIFO technique where the Last In is the First Out.

Stack is used in situations where LIFO (Last In First Out) is applicable.

Queue

This is also another type of linear data structures that is specific to two operations: addition of a component to the tail (enqueue) and extraction of the component from the head (dequeue). The two processes are fast because it utilizes a constant timing. The operations here are similar to the processes in addition and deletion of linked lists.

The Queue uses the FIFO technique where First In usually leads to the First Out. Similar to stacks, the searching and access by index is not supported by the queue. Apart from FIFO, the queue embraces the concept of **Breadth-first search (BFS).** This works by starting from the first component in the list and hence its surrounding components are aligned in a queue.

Queue is appropriate in situations where the BFS and the FIFO are applicable.

Hash table (Dictionary Implementation)

Implementation by dictionary means storage of key value and search by the latter mentioned key. The format of dictionary implementation makes the hash table to have a very fast addition, search and deletion processes. However, the hash table does not support the access by index feature because the components of the hash table have no particular order.

The components are stored in an array and located by the use of a hash function. It is also important to note that if a function is wrong, or it causes a collision of single cells then the whole implementation becomes inefficient. Hash table is the fastest data structure. This is because it provides for quick addition and searching with the use of a key.

Hash table is appropriate for a situation where fast addition is required as well as fast search by use of a key.

Hash table (Set implementation)

This data structure is a collection or grouping of components that have no duplicates. The basic processes that do happen in this data structure are the addition of components to a set, searching for the components in the set and deletion or removal of the components from the set.

This is a special kind of hash table that contains keys. It is also important to note that searching using indices is not supported. The case is similar when a bad hash function is used. When this occurs, the whole program becomes inefficient. This situation rarely occurs.

Hash table is used in situations where faster addition of components to a collection or a set is required. It is also good for checking and identification of components that do not belong to a specific data set.

Balance Tree (Dictionary Implementation)

This is a type of data structure that stores pairs of key-value where the keys used are sorted. It supports a faster operation of the addition, searching and removal processes. The algorithm complexity that is used in this data structure is logarithmic.

Collisions of functions do not affect the data structure widely as seen in hash tables. In balance trees, there is a very minimum probability of an error and usage of bad hash functions. It is very evident that in balance tree of dictionary implementation there are fast basic operations. Because of faster operations, extraction feature is enabled which is also very first with dictionary implementation.

Balance tree by dictionary implementation is used in situations where there is fast addition, searching and extraction of components that have been sorted by a particular key.

Balance tree (Set implementation)

This is a special data structure that has a red-black tree implementation where the keys and values always coincide.

Similar to the dictionary implementation, the set implementation uses the logarithmic algorithm complexity.

In summary, a balance tree by set implementation is required in situations where fast addition and checking of components is required. In addition, the components of the set are sorted in ascending order.

Practical Example of choice of a Data Structure

Example 1

In this small sub-chapter we are going to examine several examples of implemented data structures. I believe it is going to open our eyes in choices of data structures.

Our first step is to generate the subsets of a set for example;

W= {Sea, wine, computer, joy}

Our objective is to create a simple code that is going to output the subsets of W. We start from an empty set of {}. We add the empty set to each and every component of set W and we get the collection below;

{sea}, {wine}, {computer}, {joy}

Then we add to each element to the subsets from set W so that the ones which have not been included can be reflected in the two elemental subsets. There is freedom of addition up to the N-elemental subset

{sea, wine}, {sea, computer}, {sea, joy}, {wine, computer}, {wine, joy}, {computer, joy}

At this point, we are going to focus on and choose the right data structure to implement the above algorithm. In order to choose the right data structure, we are going to consider the type of operations that are needed to be done. At the moment, the main operation to be done is traversing through all the components of the set (subset). This operation can be done efficiently by the array, dynamic array, hast tables and almost all the other data structures.

i) We shall first consider the **array** because it is the simplest data structure to work with.

ii) The next step that comes after picking the data structure is to pick criterion for storing one of the 2-elemental subsets for example {beer, money}

iii) Here we check the operations which will efficiently execute this subset. The operations to be done are addition and checking of the components of the subset. From our previous knowledge, we know that arrays and linked lists perform a quicker search. We choose the data structure that is fast in addition and searching.

iv) We pick on the hash table (set implementation) and hence keep the collection or grouping of the words in the subsets as shown below;

{sea, wine}, {sea, computer}, {sea, joy}, {wine, computer}, {wine, joy}, {computer, joy}

v) Using the chosen structure, addition and traversing through the components of the subset is very efficient. At this point we get to notice that other data structures such as; stacks, Sets, queue and list also qualify for this characteristic. On the other end, if we study further we notice that this set W works with FIFO technique. At this point we choose the queue.

vi) Lastly, we obtain that queue is the best data structure for this program.

Using the queue data structure

We can illustrate and describe the algorithm using the following procedure;

i) Begin the queue with an empty set {}

ii) Dequeue the components of the subset. Add each and every element from W in relation to the subset it is located.

iii) Repeat until the queue is empty.

It is very evident that once a developer understands the needs of the program and hence selects the correct data structure, implementation becomes very quick and easy. The example below is how the program will look after applying the correct data structure;

```
string[] words = {"sea", "wine", "computer", "joy"};
Queue<HashSet<string>> subsetsQueue =new
Queue<HashSet<string>>();
HashSet<string> emptySet = new HashSet<string>();
subsetsQueue.Enqueue(emptySet);
while (subsetsQueue.Count > 0)

{
HashSet<String> subset = subsetsQueue.Dequeue();
// Display the current subset
Console.Write("{ ");
foreach (string word in subset)
{
Console.Write("{0} ", word);
}
Console.WriteLine("}");
// Generating and enqueuing all possible child subsets
foreach (string element in words)
{
if (! subset.Contains(element))
{
HashSet<string> newSubset = new HashSet<string>();
newSubset.UnionWith(subset);
newSubset.Add(element);
subsetsQueue.Enqueue(newSubset);
}
}
}
```

When the program is run through the compiler the following will be displayed;

```
{ }
{ sea }
{ wine }
{ computer }
{ joy }
{ sea wine }
{ sea computer }
{ sea joy }
{ wine sea }
...
```

Understanding our code

The coding above was successful but had one major problem. Some of the subsets of W were displayed twice. For example; {sea wine} and {wine sea} is the same subset. Our code experiences the problem of duplication.

How do we overcome duplication?

In order to overcome the problem of duplication we use indices as shown below;

```
sea → 0
wine → 1
computer → 2
joy → 3
```

In addition, we are going to generate subset using their indices in ascending order. At this point we will avoid the use of the Hash table and implement the **List.** This will place the indices in ascending order. After choosing the list, our program will look at the following;

```
using System;
using System.Collections.Generic;
public class Subsets
```

```
{
static string[] words = { "ocean", "beer", "money",
"happiness" };
static void Main()
{
Queue<List<int>> subsetsQueue = new Queue<List<int>>();
List<int> emptySet = new List<int>();
subsetsQueue.Enqueue(emptySet);
while (subsetsQueue.Count > 0)
{
List<int> subset = subsetsQueue.Dequeue();
Print(subset);
int start = -1;
if (subset.Count > 0)
{
start = subset[subset.Count - 1];

}
for (int i = start + 1; i < words.Length; i++)
{
List<int> newSubset = new List<int>();
newSubset.AddRange(subset);
newSubset.Add(i);
subsetsQueue.Enqueue(newSubset);
}
}
}
static void Print(List<int> subset) {
Console.Write("[ ");
for (int i=0; i<subset.Count; i++) {
int index = subset[i];
Console.Write("{0} ", words[index]);
}
Console.WriteLine("]");
}
}
```

After running the compiler through the program it will display the following output;

```
[ ]
[ ocean ]
[ beer ]
[ money ]
[ happiness ]
[ ocean beer ]
[ ocean money ]
[ ocean happiness ]
[ beer money ]
[ beer happiness ]
[ money happiness ]
[ ocean beer money ]
[ ocean beer happiness ]
[ ocean money happiness ]
[ beer money happiness ]
[ ocean beer money happiness ]
```

Example 2- Sorting the numbers in a phonebook

Here we have a file containing texts that have people's credentials such as their names, the cities they live in and their cell phone numbers. The table below shows the information;

Names	Cities	Cell Phone Numbers
Kennedy	Nairobi	1-234-567-8911
Silas	Lusaka	2-345-678-9112
Joseph	Jerusalem	3-456-789-1112
Diana	Kisumu	4-567-891-2345
Winston	Migori	5-678-912-3456

Task: *Write a code which displays all the* **names of the cities in alphabetical order** *and for each one of them prints all* **the names of the people in alphabetical order** *and their corresponding* **phone numbers**.

There are many solutions for such an example illustrated in the table above. We are going to utilize the knowledge we have learned in the previous topics about data structures to solve this problem. We shall use the examples of data structures in the Dot Net Framework.

From the requirements of the codes, we need to sort the names of the cities. This makes us open our line of thoughts towards the data structures that can make us achieve the sorting criterion. For this case we can consider a balanced tree either set implementation or dictionary implementation. However, the records of the phonebook also contain the names of the city and hence we have to use dictionary implementation. As a result, the list containing the names of people will be kept with their respective cell phone numbers. We will initialize the key to be the names of the people and the value to be their respective phone numbers

The following is an illustration of the program using dictionary implementation;

```
// Read the file and build the phone book
SortedDictionary<string, SortedDictionary<string, string>>
phonesByTown = new SortedDictionary<string,
SortedDictionary<string, string>>();
StreamReader reader = new StreamReader("PhoneBook.txt");
using (reader)
{
while (true)
{
```

```csharp
string line = reader.ReadLine();
if (line == null)
{
break;

}
string[] entry = line.Split(new char[]{'|'});
string name = entry[0].Trim();
string town = entry[1].Trim();
string phone = entry[2].Trim();
SortedDictionary<string, string> phoneBook;
if (! phonesByTown.TryGetValue(town, out phoneBook))
{
// This town is new. Create a phone book for it
phoneBook = new SortedDictionary<string, string>();
phonesByTown.Add(town, phoneBook);
}
phoneBook.Add(name, phone);
}
}
// Print the phone book by towns
foreach (string town in phonesByTown.Keys)
{
Console.WriteLine("Town " + town + ":");
SortedDictionary<string, string> phoneBook =
phonesByTown[town];
foreach (var entry in phoneBook)
{
string name = entry.Key;
string phone = entry.Value;
Console.WriteLine("\t{0} - {1}", name, phone);
}
}
```

If the code were run by the compiler, the following would be the appropriate display;

Town Portland:
Mary - 1-234-765-1983
Town San Antonio:
Laura - 1-454-345-2345
Paul - 1-535-675-6745
Town Virginia Beach:
Donna - 1-387-387-2389
Kenneth - 1-541-754-3010

Summary (How to choose an appropriate Data structure)

At this point of learning, it is very evident that the choice of data structure is dependent on the objective of the program to be written. On another occasion, we noted that we could combine data structures in order to achieve specific unique situations and results.

Before choosing a particular data structure, it is important that one asks him or herself several questions. The questions include;

- What operations will I perform in my program?

- The operation to be performed requires which type of structure?

- Am I familiar with all the data structures that exist in C# programming language?

- Does my program require a single data structure or a combination of two or three?

In conclusion, the choice of data structure is an important step. It is advised that before you choose a particular data structure you should design an algorithm. Never start by choosing the data structure back to the algorithm.

Chapter Five

Control Statements, Loops and Conditions

Introduction

In the programming world there exist a lot of things and factors that make the program coding to become a success. In C# programming language, the instructions that are formulated are designed to be of a high-level language. These are very advanced codes that simulate various loops and control statements hence achieve a high level of skill.

In C# programming language, there are three types of high-level statements. These statements make the programmer or developer work under a high level of skill and abstraction. The three types of high-level statements include;

a) **Input/output high-level statement**

   Input statements are the type of statements that take up values from the computer user for manipulation in the program
   Output statements are the type of statements that displays the result of manipulation inside the computer program

b) **Assignment statement**-this is similar to the input statement except for the fact that it does not collect anything from the computer user. The main function of the assignment statement is the assigning of values to the program variables.

c) **Control statements**- this type of statements completely affect the computer's operations. The control statements usually direct the control flow of a program from the beginning to the end.

Definition of other statements in C# Programming language

- **Iteration statements** are those statements that help in the creation of loops in a program using specific keywords like *foreach, for, do* and *while*.

- **Jump statements** are statements that are used especially in transferring the program controls by utilizing specific keywords like *return, break, continue* and *yield.*

- **Exception-handling statements** are statements that are majorly used to handle unique or exception cases using keywords such as *try-catch, throw, try-catch-finally* and *try-finally.*

In this chapter, we are going to focus more on the control statements basing our discussion and studies in the loops. The learner should be very keen to note the differences between the control statements and hence know how to implement the statements.

Control Statements

There are three types of control statement mechanisms that are used in C# programming language;

i) Sequential mechanism- these include instructions that are organized and executed in a definite order

ii) Conditional mechanism- the instructions that are executed here are dependents on conditions.

iii) Looping mechanism- the instructions that exist here can be executed repeatedly.

In the whole chapter we have been using a sequential mechanism. In this topic, we are going to put more focus on conditional and looping mechanisms.

Conditional statements

As defined before, these are the kind of statements that execute instructions depending on some stated conditions. Examples of conditional statements that exist in the C# programming language include;

    a. IF statement

    b. Switch

The If Statement

It is very important to notice that the structure of If statement that is used in C# programming language shares the same syntax as of those that are used in other programming languages such as Java, C++ and C programming languages. The syntax is as shown below;

if-statement ::= "if" "(" condition ")" if-body ["else" else-body]

condition ::= boolean-expression
if-body ::= statement-or-statement-block
else-body ::= statement-or-statement-block

Understanding our syntax

The If statement relies on the parent condition in order for it to execute the command in the body syntax. An "else" phrase always follows after the body syntax is executed and is usually applicable when the condition returns a false value. It is important to note that the "else" phrase can be cascaded to "nested if". The following is an example of an IF statement program in C# programming language;

```
using System;
public class IfStatementSample
{
public void IfMyNumberIs()
{
int myNumber = 5;
if ( myNumber == 4 )
Console.WriteLine("This will not be shown because myNumber is not
4.");
else if( myNumber < 0 )
{
Console.WriteLine("This will not be shown because myNumber is not
negative.");
}
else if( myNumber % 2 == 0 )
Console.WriteLine("This will not be shown because myNumber is not
even.");
else
{
Console.WriteLine("myNumber does not match the coded conditions,
so this sentence will be shown!");
}
}
}
```

Switch Statement

Likewise, the switch statements shares similarities with the syntax of Java, C++ and C Programming language. However, in C Programming language the statements are supposed to finish with jump statements as opposed to C# programming language. The following is a good example of a switch case program in C programming language;

```
switch (nCPU)
{
case 0:
Console.WriteLine("You don't have a CPU! :-)");
break;
case 1:
Console.WriteLine("Single processor computer");
break;
case 2:
Console.WriteLine("Dual processor computer");
break;
// Stacked cases
case 3:
case 4:
case 5:
case 6:
case 7:
case 8:
Console.WriteLine("A multi processor computer");
break;
default:
Console.WriteLine("A seriously parallel computer");
break;
}
```

Understanding our code

The code above is a code written in C programming language. A jump statement "break" has been used at the end of each code as opposed to C# programming language. Another property that has been used and is very much allowed is stacking. Stacking is used for reference for example goto case 1.

The program below shows advancement in C# programming language by the use of a string which is a switch variable;

```
switch (aircraft_ident)
{
case "C-FESO":
Console.WriteLine("Rans S6S Coyote");
break;
case "C-GJIS":
Console.WriteLine("Rans S12XL Airaile");
break;
default:
Console.WriteLine("Unknown aircraft");
break;
}
```

Looping Statements

A loop can be defined as a repeated execution of a portion of source code. There exist two types of loops; finite and infinite loops.

Infinite loops can be defined as those loops that never come to an end while those loops that have a terminal end are referred to as finite loops. We are going to discuss the following types of loops; *while loop, do-while loop, for loop* and *for-each loop.*

In this topic we are going to discuss various ways to create loops.

The While loop

The while loop has a similar syntax compared to all the other programming languages that were derived from the C Language. The syntax is as shown below;

while-loop ::= "while" "(" condition ")" body
condition ::= boolean-expression
body ::= statement-or-statement-block

This is similar to;

```
while (condition)
{
looping body;
}
```

Understanding our code;

The condition above includes a Boolean expression that requires a *yes/no or true/false* result. It basically dictates the duration in which the looping body will be continuously repeated. The Looping body can be explained as the platform where the execution of the programmed code takes place.

In a while loop, the result of the Boolean expression is determined if it true before the looping process begins. The basis of the looping is to determine the point at which the condition becomes false and the program stops. At special cases, the looping body may not be executed if the first condition that is tested in a false result. The following is a simple example of the while loop;

```
// Initialize the counter
int counter = 0;
// Execute the loop body while the loop condition holds
```

```
while (counter <= 9)
{
// Print the counter value
Console.WriteLine("Number : " + counter);
// Increment the counter
counter++;
}
```

When the compiler executes the program it will display the following;

```
Number : 0
Number : 1
Number : 2
Number : 3
Number : 4
Number : 5
Number : 6
Number : 7
Number : 8
Number : 9
```

NOTE: The operator break is a feature that is used for the premature exit of a loop. This happens in a situation where the loop must come to an end before it is completely executed. It can only be done from the body of the program. When the operator break is executed the next line of code will be skipped hence not executed. The following is an example of a short program that illustrates the use of the operator break;

```
int n = int.Parse(Console.ReadLine());
// "decimal" is the biggest C# type that can hold integer values
decimal factorial = 1;
// Perform an "infinite loop"
while (true)
{
```

```
if (n <= 1)
{

break;
}
factorial *= n;
n--;
}
Console.WriteLine("n! = " + factorial);
```

Understanding the Code

The example is about a program that calculates the factorial of any number that is input. The program is implemented using an operator break and the infinite form of the while loop.

The Do-while loop

This type of loop is almost same to the while loop except that it performs a check on the condition each and every time an execution takes place. It is sometimes referred to as the "post-test" loop. The syntax for the do-while loop is similar to that in C programming language;

```
do...while-loop ::= "do" body "while" "(" condition ")"
condition ::= boolean-expression
body ::= statement-or-statement-block
```

This is also similar to the following code in a program;

```
do
{
executable code;
} while (condition);
```

Understanding our code

The do-while loop usually runs through its looping body just once. After the initial running through the code, it examines the condition whether it needs to run through the body for the second time. If the condition turns to be true, the execution of the body is done. The same process is repeated until the result of the examination becomes false then it terminates the loop. The following is an example of a sample program of a do-while loop.

```
using System;
public class DoWhileLoopExample
{
    public void PrintValuesBetweenTenAndZero()
    {
      int number = 0;
      do
       {
       Console.WriteLine(number++.ToString());
       } while(number <= 10);
    }
}
```

The above code displays the integers within a 0-10 range.

The For-loop

These types of loops are slightly complex than the while and the do-while loops. This is because they are designed to perform more complex situations as compared to the two previous loops. The same applies to the syntax that exists in the C programming language;

```
for-loop ::= "for" "(" initialization ";" condition ";" iteration ")" body
initialization ::= variable-declaration | list-of-statements
condition ::= boolean-expression
```

iteration ::= list-of-statements
body ::= statement-or-statement-block

This is also similar to the following code in a program;

```
for (initialization; condition; update)
{
loop's body;
}
```

Understanding our code

For this loop, initialization is done first since the statements are executed through the loop. This is done for declaration and initialization of the program purpose. The expression that holds the condition is usually examined before going through to determine if the body is executable. This loop is usually applied to test for limits. For instance, when the condition becomes true, the body becomes executable. The following is an example of a program illustrating the for-loop;

```
public class ForLoopExample
{
  public void ForFirstHundredNaturalNumbers()
  {
    for(int i=0; i<100; i++)
    {
      System.Console.WriteLine(i.ToString());
    }
  }
}
```

The code written above displays the integers between 0 and 99.

The Foreach-loop

This is a new development in this C# programming language. It was common in Visual Basic and PHP programming languages. This loop is known to pass through all the elements in a specific collection such as an array. This happens even when the array or the collection does not have an index search. The syntax for this loop is illustrated below;

```
foreach-loop ::= "foreach" "(" variable-declaration "in" enumerable-
expression ")" body
body ::= statement-or-statement-block
```

This is also similar to the following code in a program;

```
foreach (type variable in collection)
{
statements;
}
```

Understanding our code

In this code, the "enumerable-expression" is an expression that is used to implement the **IEnumerable** so that an array can be established. Secondly, the "variable declaration" is used in the declaration of variables which will be set as successive components of the array. The following is an example of a program that implements the foreach-loop;

```
public class ForEachExample
{
  public void PerformAnActionOnEachItem()
  {
  string[] itemsToWrite = {"Clinton", "Brian", "Charles"};
  foreach (string item in itemsToWrite)
   System.Console.WriteLine(item);
```

```
      }
   }
```

The program runs through the array and displays the names above.

The Nested Loops

These are programming codings that are made up of several types of loops which work together. It works with a principle where the innermost used code is the most repeated and executed. The syntax of the nested loops is shown below;

```
for (initialization, verification, update)
{
for (initialization, verification, update)
{

executable code
} ...
}
```

Understanding our code

After the first for-loop is initialized, the body begins to be executed which has the nested-loop. The variable undergoes initialization which enables the condition to be checked and hence the body becomes executed. The execution of the body will continue until the condition becomes false. The program below is a simple illustration that prints a triangle using numbers;

```
int x = int.Parse(Console.ReadLine());
for (int row = 1; row <= x; row++)
{
for (int col = 1; col <= row; col++)
{
Console.Write(col + " ");
```

```
}
Console.WriteLine();
}
```

```
        Its output will become;

    1
    1 2
    1 2 3
    1 2 3 4
    1 2 3 4 5
    1 2 3 4 5 6
    1 2 3 4 5 6 7
```

Chapter Six

Arrays in C Sharp Programming Language

In this chapter, we shall discuss arrays in deep and know how they coordinate and work with the sequences of components of the same caliber.

We are going to define, create, and declare and know how to use the arrays. There are several types of arrays some of which are either one dimensional or multi-dimensional.

Definition

An array can be defined as a collection of several variables which are referred to as elements or components. Arrays in the C# programming language can be numbered and referred to as **indices**. The numbers of components of arrays are collectively known as the **length of the array**.

The components of a single array are usually of the same type and manner. This type of grouping is done in order to allow the programmer to represent a number of similar elements as ordered sequences.

As mentioned before, the array can either be one dimensional or multi-dimensional. The other name for one-dimensional arrays is known **as vectors** whereas the other name for multi-dimensional arrays is **matrices.**

Declaration and Allocating declared Arrays

Declaration of an Array

In the C# programming language, all the arrays have a fixed length. It is important to notice that once the length of an array has been set it cannot be reset.

The following is a syntax that is used in the declaration of an array in the C# programming language;

    int[] AnArray;

The piece of code above shows that the **TheArray** is the name of the array containing integer (Int []). The square brackets above are used to show that the array is not a single element but a collection of components. When an array is usually declared, it depends whether it's a reference or a value. The reference arrays are achieved when the array's variable lacks values. This means that the memory is not allocated for the values.

Creating an Array

In the C# programming language, a new array is created by the use of the keyword **"new"**. It also takes part in the allocation of memory to the newly created array. The following is the syntax for creating a new array;

    int [] TheArray = new int[8];

The piece of code above shows that an array has been allocated a length of seven which are integers (Int []). This means that the memory allocated for the array is eight integers which are initialized at value zero.

The dynamic memory is also known as the heap memory. During the allocation of the memory of the array, there is no negative number that is considered.

Initialization of Arrays and Allocation of Default Values

The components of an array are set usually to be manipulated or used for some reason. Before the components of the array are used, they are initialized and given default values. In the C# programming language, it is a must that all the components of a given array which have also been initialized have a default initial value. This value is usually a zero for the numeral figures. The following is a simple example;

```
int[] TheArray = { 1, 2, 3, 4, 5, 6 };
```

The following is an example of how we can declare and initialize an array;

```
string[] daysOfWeek =
{ "Monday", "Tuesday", "Wednesday", "Thursday", "Friday",
"Saturday", "Sunday" };
```

Understanding our code

In the above example, the array contains seven components that are a string type. This means that the components of the array are of reference type. The array is allocated back to the stack memory.

Boundaries of the Array

The default values of arrays begin from zero. Using mathematical expression, this means that in an array having M components then the last component has the index (N-1).

In order to access the components of an array, we use the indices. For a programmer to access a component he must access the component through an array's name and its index number usually enclosed in a bracket. The following is a good example of accessing an array;

TheArray[index] = 300;// a value equating to 300 has been initialized to the element located at the position index.

The following is another example where an array is allocated some numbers and at a point they are changed;

```
int[] myArray = new int[7];
myArray[1] = 2;
myArray[5] = 6;
```

Let use the for-loop to change the initials and change the memory allocation as shown below;

```
int[] arr = new int[6];
for (int i = 0; i < arr.Length; i++)
{
arr[i] = i;
}
```

Traversing the Boundaries of an Array

In the C# programming language, the Dot Net framework is very strict in checking the access done to components of an array. This is achieved by the use of the code **System.IndexOutOfRangeException** which helps the programmers to identify the possibility of errors in the code. However, this procedure happens to interrupt and affect the general performance of a code or a program. The following is an example of a traverse of a boundary of an array;

```
class TheArrayReverseExample
{
static void Main()
{
int[] array = { 2, 3, 4, 5, 6 };
// Find the array size
int length = array.Length;
// Declaration and creation of the reversed array
int[] reversed = new int[length];
// Initialization of the reversed array
for (int index = 0; index < length; index++)
{
reversed[length - index - 1] = array[index];
}

// Printing of the reversed array
for (int index = 0; index < length; index++)
{
Console.Write(reversed[index] + " ");
}
}
}
}
// Output: 6 5 4 3 2
```

Understanding our code

The example above depicts the following concept: initially there was an allocation of a one-dimensional array of the integer type. It was initialized it with the numbers from one to five. After that, the length of the array was kept in the **"variable length"**. It is very important to note that we are utilizing the property **Length**. This returns the collective total result of the components of the array. In C# programming language, each and every array have a length property. After the declaration of the reversed array with the same **length**, the elements of the original array are kept in a reversed manner. To reverse the components, we will use a **for**-loop. After each loop, we increase the **index** variable by one. The access to each and every consecutive elements of the **array is enabled**. The loop condition will always ensure that the array will continue to work in the loop from one end to another.

Let's follow the incidences that happen when we continue looping through the **array**. During the first loop, the **index** has a value of 0. Using **array [index]**, we first access the first element of the **array. Later,** with **reversed [length - index - 1]**, we access the last component of the new array **reversed** where we assign the values. Thus, we appropriated the value of the first component of the **array** to the last component of the **reversed** array. At each looping, the **index** is increased by one. This way, we access the next component in the order of **array** and the previous component in the order of **reversed**. As a result we reversed the array and printed it. In the example we showed consecutive looping through the array, which can also be done with different types of loop constructs.

Identification of Arrays (Reading of Arrays)

One of the ways of achieving this is to read the arrays or the values of the arrays using a console. In most cases, the reading of an array from a console is achieved through the use of the Dot Net framework accessories as well as the for-loop.

From the beginning, the reading was done using a console for example; Console.ReadLine () which was later followed by a parse to the integer type and finally set to a specific variable. The number specified by the variable was later used as the length of the array as shown below;

```
int n = int.Parse(Console.ReadLine());
int[] array = new int[n];
```

Afterwards, a loop was carried out on the array. The current element that is obtained from the looping is initialized by every reading from the console. The number of the loop will go up to the number equal to the length of the arrays. This means it will go through each and every element of the array as shown below;

```
for (int i = 0; i < n; i++)
{
array[i] = int.Parse(Console.ReadLine());
}
```

The following is a general example of reading of the array from the console;

```
Console.Write("Input a positive integer: ");
int n = int.Parse(Console.ReadLine());
int[] array = new int[n];
Console.WriteLine("Input the values of the array:");
for (int i = 0; i < n; i++)
{
array[i] = int.Parse(Console.ReadLine());
}
bool symmetric = true;
for (int i = 0; i < array.Length / 2; i++)
{
if (array[i] != array[n - i - 1])
{
symmetric = false;
break;
}
}
Console.WriteLine("Is it symmetric? {0}", symmetric);
```

The above example is a program that checks for any symmetric array. A symmetric array is that array which contains the first and the last components equal and the same.

Printing an Array to the Display

This is usually done when all the manipulation has been done on the array. There are no strict rules for the printing of arrays. However, a certain criterion for formatting is largely applied for the printing to the console. The for loop is used to print the components of the array as shown below;

```
string[] array = { "two", "three", "four", "five" };
for (int index = 0; index < array.Length; index++)
{
// Printing of every element in a separate line
Console.WriteLine("Element[{0}] = {1}", index, array[index]);
}
```

Understanding our code

The for-loop performs the looping during the printing up to a number of times equal to the length of the array. The print will be applicable to applying the **Console.WriteLine()and the formatted string** as shown below;

```
Element[1] = two
Element[2] = three
Element[3] = four
Element[4] = five
```

Multidimensional types of arrays

As mentioned before, the one-dimensional arrays are referred to as *vectors* whereas the multi-dimensional arrays are referred to as *matrices*. This would lead us to inquire and get to know more about the matrices and maybe explain about their applications.

Definition of Matrices

It is important to note that any valid type that exists in C# programming language can be applied as any type of array. This means that we can also have "arrays of arrays". This also means that vectors and matrices can be declared uniquely.

For instance, vectors are declared by use of **int []** whereas the matrices are declared by the use of **int [,]**. The example below shows the unique type of declaration among vectors and matrices;

```
int[,] twoDimensionalArray;// for two dimensional array.
int[,,] threeDimensionalArray;// for three dimensional array.
```

NOTE: *We are going to refer to the matrices as multidimensional arrays for the sake of programming because the "matrices" name is a mathematical term.*

Declaring and Allocation of Multi-dimensional Array

The declaration and allocation of multi-dimensional arrays happen the same as those of one-dimensional arrays. However, the only unique thing is the addition of commas while marking the dimensions of the arrays as shown below;

```
int[,] intMatrix;
float[,] floatMatrix;
string[,,] strCube;
```

Understanding our code

In the example above we have a creation of 2-dimensional and 3-dimensional type of arrays which are shown by the markings of the commas. After the declaration, we allocate memory to the arrays. This is achieved by the use of the keyword "**new**" which is done for each dimension using a set length.

The following is an example of how memory is allocated;

```
int[,] intMatrix = new int[4, 5];
float[,] floatMatrix = new float[7, 3];
string[,,] stringCube = new string[6, 6, 6];
```

Understanding our example

The intMatrix is a 2-dimensional matrix that contains three components which are integers (Int []). The three components have a length equated to four.

Initializing a 2-Dimensional Array

The procedure for initializing a 2-Dimensional array is the same as the one used in initializing a one-dimensional array as illustrated below;

```
int[,] matrix =
{
{2, 3, 4, 5}, // row 0 values
{6, 7, 8, 9}, // row 1 values
};
// The size of the matrix is 2 x 4 (2 rows, 4 cols)
```

Understanding our code

After the initialization of the 2-dimensional array having integer type with 4 columns and 2rows, we use the outer brackets to assist us in placing the components belonging to the first dimension.

Multi-dimensional Arrays Length

In the C# programming language, each matrix bears its own unique length. The length is mostly used for purposes of accessing the codes during the running of the lines of codes (Execution).

The following is an example of a 2-dimensional array;

```
int[,] matrix =
{
{2, 3, 4, 5},
{6, 7, 8, 9},
};
```

Understanding our code

It is possible to know the number of rows and columns in the example above by use of library line of codes which we will state below. For you to get the number of rows we use **matrix.GetLength(0)** whereas for the columns we use **matrix.GetLength(1)** which will return 2 and 4 respectively.

The following is an example of how 2-dimensional arrays can be printed;

```
// Declaration and initialization of the matrix of size 2 x 4
int[,] matrix =
{
{2, 3, 4, 5}, // row 0 values
{6, 7, 8, 9}, // row 1 value
};
// Printing of the matrix on the console
    for (int row = 0; row < matrix.GetLength(0); row++)
    {
        for (int col = 0; col < matrix.GetLength(1); col++)
        {
```

```
        Console.Write(matrix[row, col]);
    }
    Console.WriteLine();
}
```

Understanding our code

In the example above, in order to print a matrix you have to declare and initialize the array. After a couple of looping by use of For-loop the array is printed.

Arrays of arrays

They are also referred to as "**Jagged arrays**". They can be defined as arrays of arrays because each of their rows has a unique array amongst itself. The array within the array is allowed to have a different length from the ones in the initial rows.

Declaring and Allocating Memory to Jagged Arrays

There is a difference in the declaration of multi-dimensional arrays and jagged arrays. The major difference between the two is the use of multiple brackets as compared to a single pair of brackets used by multi-dimensional arrays. In simple terms, the array of arrays uses a pair of brackets in each dimension just as shown below;

```
int[][] jaggedArray;
jaggedArray = new int[3][];
jaggedArray[0] = new int[6];
jaggedArray[1] = new int[4];
```

In addition, we will use the example below to illustrate the declaration, allocation and initialization of jagged arrays with integer components:

```
int[][] myJaggedArray = {
new int[] {6, 8, 3},
new int[] {11, 21, 41},
new int[] {4, 26}
};
```

Allocation of Memory to Jagged Arrays

Jagged arrays can be referred to as a compilation of references. It is important to notice that the jagged arrays do not have arrays pointing directly to them but the components of the arrays are the ones which are directly pointing to the compilation of references. When the allocation of memory is done, the references begin to work directly by pointing to the dynamic memory.

Access to the components

This is achieved by the use of indices. In the example below, the components will be accessed by index 3 of the jagged array.

```
myJaggedArray[1][3] = 46;
```

In addition, the components of the arrays of arrays can either be vectors or matrices. The illustration below shows jagged arrays containing components of 2-dimensional arrays;

```
int[][,] jaggedOfMulti = new int[2][,];
jaggedOfMulti[0] = new int[,] { { 5, 15 }, { 125, 206 } };
jaggedOfMulti[1] = new int[,] { { 3, 4, 5 }, { 7, 8, 9 } };
```

Practical exercises

1. Write a program, which creates an array of **20 elements of type integer** and initializes each of the elements with a value equals to the index of the element multiplied by 5. Print the elements to the console.

2. Write a program, which **reads two arrays** from the console and **checks whether they are equal** (two arrays are equal when they are of equal length and all of their elements, which have the same index, are equal).

3. Write a program, which creates an array of **20 elements of type integer** and initializes each of the elements with a value equals to the index of the element multiplied by 5. Print the elements to the console.

4. Write a program, which **reads two arrays** from the console and **checks whether they are equal** (two arrays are equal when they are of equal length and all of their elements, which have the same index, are equal).

5. Write a program, which reads an array of integer numbers from the console and **removes a minimal number of elements** in such a way that **the remaining array is sorted** in increasing order.
Example: {6, **1**, 4, **3**, 0, **3**, 6, **4**, **5**} → {1, 3, 3, 4, 5}

6. Write a program, which reads the integer numbers **N** and **K** from the console and prints **all variations of K elements of the numbers in the interval [1...N]**. Example: N = 3, K = 2 → {1, 1}, {1, 2}, {1, 3}, {2, 1}, {2, 2}, {2, 3}, {3, 1}, {3, 2}, {3, 3}

7. Write a program, which finds the **maximal sequence of increasing elements** in an array **arr[n]**. It is not necessary the elements to be consecutively placed. E.g.: {9, 6, **2**, 7, **4**, 7, **6**, 5, **8**, 4} → {2, 4, 6, 8}.

8. Write a program, which reads from the console two integer numbers **N** and **K** (K<N) and array of N integers. Find those **K consecutive elements** in the array, which have **maximal sum**.

9. **Sorting an array** means to arrange its elements in an increasing (or decreasing) order. Write a program, which sorts an array using the algorithm "**selection sort**".

10. Write a program, which **compares two arrays of type char lexicographically** (character by character) and checks, which one is first in the lexicographical order.

11. Write a program, which finds the **maximal sequence of consecutive equal elements** in an array. E.g.: {1, 1, 2, 3, **2, 2, 2**, 1} → {2, 2, 2}.

12. Write a program, which finds the **maximal sequence** of consecutively placed **increasing** integers. Example: {3, **2, 3, 4**, 2, 2, 4} → {2, 3, 4}

Chapter Seven

Methods and Recursions

In this chapter we are going to study two major components used in C# programming language. These are methods and recursions. We shall consider them independently.

Definition and importance of methods

In this subtopic we are going to interact with methods, where to use them, declaration of methods, calling a method and the body of the method. The learning of the methods will be accompanied by exercises and examples that will assist us in understanding the methods deeper.

In a simple definition, methods are defined as a very central (basic) part of a program. This is because it is able to solve a problem by the input of parameters and output of a result. It usually consists of the logic and expressions of the main program. The method can be taken as a nerve part of a very large program and can act as an avenue for creating and building other bigger programs.

Methods apply the concept of subroutines for them to achieve a purpose. In a nutshell, the subroutine uses the principle of dividing and conquering. This is by dividing a bigger problem into smaller parts and then solving them and combining the solutions to achieve success.

In other programming languages, the subroutines are referred to as procedures or methods. In the C# programming languages the subroutines are generally referred to as methods.

The following is an example of a simple method that performs the calculation of the area of a rectangle;

```
static double CalculateRectangleArea(double width, double height)
{
double area = width * height;
return area;
}
```

What is the importance of methods?

There are so many reasons why many programmers prefer to use methods. Each and every person who has had experience with methods can explain the importance differently. I believe that when you gain experience in the C# programming you will use your own words to explain. The following are some of the importance of methods;

1. Highly structured and Readable program

   Methods make the program to have a better structure and can be easily read by another person. This makes the program neat and can be understood by other programmers as well. On the other end, the program becomes easy to maintain and correct the errors. In addition, it makes it viable for advancement and addition of new features to the written line of codes.

2. Avoids Duplication of Codes

   Methods help the programmer to avoid repetition of line codes. This is because the methods were highly designed using the concept of "**Code Reuse'**.

3. "Code Reuse"

This concept applies best when a line of code has been used two times or more in the same program. A method can be used to separate such line of codes which have been used more than once. The method allows the programmer to reuse the same line of code without rewriting the code. On the other end, it makes the programmer avoid repetition of the same code as well as make the program well structured.

Declaration and implementation of methods

Declaration of a method can be referred to as registering of a method in a program in order to identify the method in the program. On the other end, implementation is the same as the creation of a logical expression that solves a particular problem.

A method call can be described as a procedure of reference to a declared method in the middle of solving a particular problem.

Before the programmer declares any method, he or she is entitled to know appropriate places where a declaration of methods is required.

NOTE: *In C# programming language, methods are declared between two specific points which are the opening and closing brackets enclosing a class."{}".*

The following is an example of the explanation of above;

```
public class HiCSharp
{
// Opening the braces of the class
```

```
// Declaration of the method existing between the class' body braces
static void Main(string[] args)
{
Console.WriteLine("Hi CSharp!");
}
} // Closing of the braces of the class
```

After we have known and understood the appropriate places where to declare a method, we are ready to declare the method. A method can be declared as shown below;

[static] <return_type> <method_name>([<param_list>])

In order to appropriately declare a method, there are regulations that must be followed which include;

- The type of output gained by the method

- The name of the method

- The list of all the parameters back to the method.

In summary, during the declaration of a method, the first component to be considered is the return value of the method, followed by the name of the method and the last is always the list having the parameters enclosed in the round brackets. It is important to note that the round brackets are usually used immediately after the name of the method. This is regardless of any situation such as lack of parameters.

The method signature

This is a component that is used in the identification of methods mostly in object-oriented programming. It is at times called the method specification since it consists of a pair of elements such as the method names and the list containing the parameters.

In C# programming language, the method is identified by its unique signature. However, the return value of the method is not a component of the method signature. This explains the confusion between two methods having different return values and which one should be called instead of the other.

The Method Names

The names of the method are used mostly when the method is to be called. Whenever a particular method is called, the name of the method is typed and the values in existence are passed. The example below is an illustration;

```
static void PrintTheLogo()
{
Console.WriteLine("Google");
Console.WriteLine("www.google.com");
}
```

In order to name a method appropriately, the following rules are applied;

- The name of the method should describe the purpose of the method.

- The name of the method should always start with a capital letter.

- The rule of *"Pascalcase"* should be applied.

- The name of the method should have a verb or combination of a verb and a noun.

NOTE: *The rule of Pascalcase states that each word that is new and concatenates in the formation of a method name must always begin with an upper case letter.*

The Method's Body

The body of the method can be described as the line of code found inside the curly brackets. It comes immediately after the declaration of a method as illustrated below;

```
static <return_type> <method_name>(<parameters_list>)
{
// ... the code comes here –which is in the method's body ...
}
```

The example above shows the general skeleton format of a method. As mentioned before, the logical expression and algorithm are situated inside the method. The example below shows a body of a working method;

```
static void ThePrintLogo()
{ // the body of the method begins here
Console.WriteLine("Google");
Console.WriteLine("www.google.com");
} // ... It finishes off here.
```

In summary, it is important to note that a method should not be declared inside the body of another existing method.

Practical Exercises

1. Write a code that by given name prints on the console **"Hello, <name>!"** (for example: **"Hello, Peter!"**).

2. Create a method **GetMax()** with two integer (**int**) parameters, that returns **maximal** of the two numbers. Write a program that reads three numbers from the console and prints the biggest of them. Use the **GetMax()** method you just created. Write a test program that validates

   that the methods work correctly.

3. Write a method that returns the **English name of the last digit** of a given number. Example: for **512** prints **"two"**; for **1024** → **"four"**.

4. Write a method that finds **how many times a certain number can be found in a given array**. Write a program to test that the method works correctly.

5. Write a method that checks whether an element, from a certain position in an array is **greater than its two neighbors**. Test whether the method works correctly.

Recursion

In this subtopic, we are going to learn about recursions and its areas of application. This can be defined as a very powerful technique in programming where the method is able to call itself from its own body. We are going to learn other features that make the process above possible such as the generation of variations and permutations using examples and illustrations.

The use of recursion becomes powerful upon correct usage and can produce very complex results that are elegant and unique in nature. The other major functions of recursions include the simplification of the line of codes and making the lines of codes easily readable.

In order to learn more about recursions we will use an illustrative example of Fibonacci numbers. the following numbers are examples of Fibonacci numbers

1, 1, 2, 3, 5, 8, 13, 21, 34, 55, 89, 144,

From our simple mathematics we will notice that the sequence is formed by adding the first initial numbers in the series. The formula shown below will be used to develop the sequence;

$F1 = F2 = 1$
$Fi = Fi\text{-}1 + Fi\text{-}2 \text{ (for } i > 2)$

The following is an implementation of the recursion method that will be used to calculate the next number in the Fibonacci series;

```
using System;
class TheRecursiveFibonacciCalculation
{
    static long[] numbers;
    static void Main()
    {
    Console.Write("x = ");
    int x = int.Parse(Console.ReadLine());
    numbers = new long[n + 2];
    numbers[1] = 1;
    numbers[2] = 1;
    long result = Fib(x);
    Console.WriteLine("fib({0}) = {1}", x, result);
    }
```

```
    static long Fib(int x)
    {
if (0 == numbers[x])
    {
    numbers[x] = Fib(x - 1) + Fib(x - 2);
    }
    return numbers[x];
    }
    }
```

Understanding our Code

The example above is a simple illustration of how recursion works. On the other hand, we have to learn to be very sensitive in the application of recursion. In other cases, recursion can be used wrongly and lead to ambiguous results. The following is a short example of the wrong use of recursion that leads to inefficiency.

```
    static long Fib(int n)
    {
if (n <= 2)
    {
    return 1;
    }
    return Fib(n - 1) + Fib(n - 2);
    }
```

Types of recursions

At this point we have two types of recursions. It includes the direct recursions and the indirect recursions.

A direct recursion is achieved when a call is made by the body of the method existing within the same method. An indirect or mutual recursion is when method X calls method Y and method Y calls method Z and method Z calls method X. this depicts a channel of calls where methods call other methods in order to achieve the final purpose.

Recursion Bottom Cases

In a recursion procedure, it is appropriate that after several steps there is an accurate result or return. In cases where the accurate result is obtained without conducting a recursive call or procedure is called the **"bottom of recursion"**.

For instance, the bottom of recursion in the calculation of the Fibonacci series is when the result is less than or equivalent to two. If the recursive call cannot result in a base case then the bottom becomes infinite.

Creation of Recursive methods

In order for the creation of recursion methods to be successful we have to borrow from the subroutine concept. This means we have to use the divide and conquer technique to divide big tasks into smaller tasks in order to solve them in bits. The collective solutions from the small tasks should be able to be the solution to the big initial task.

In this case we will have to apply the bottom of recursion case until the final return is achieved for each and every bit of divided task.

We will utilize an example of factorial in order to understand the concept of creation of recursion methods.

The factorial of a value x is calculated by finding the product of all existing numbers between 1 and x. the numbers should be integers and the last value is the number x as shown below;

x! = 1.2.3...x

The solution to the calculation is accurately done when the corresponding definition of recurring factorial is used.

x! = 1, for x = 0
x! = x.(x-1)!, for x>0

Understanding our code

For finding factorial, we need to calculate for the formula of recurrent dependability in order to achieve the solution for the tasks that will have to reach the bottom of recursion. For example the recurring dependability to reach the bottom of recursion for factorial is as shown below;

x! = x.(x-1)!

We have to apply the bottom of recursion having the simplest case as zero and the starting value for the factorial to be one. The program below shows the method which satisfies the conditions and hence calculates for the factorial;

```
using System;
class TheRecursiveFactorial
{
static void Main()
{
Console.Write("x = ");
int x = int.Parse(Console.ReadLine());
decimal factorial = Factorial(x);
Console.WriteLine("{0}! = {1}", x, factorial);
}
static decimal Factorial(int x)
{
// This is the bottom of the recursion
```

```
if (x == 0)
{
return 1;
}
// Recursive call: the method calls itself
else
{
return x * Factorial(x - 1);
}
}
}
```

Practical Exercises

1. Write a program to simulate n nested loops from 1 to n.

2. Write a program to generate all variations with duplicates of n elements class k. Sample input: n = 3 k = 2 Sample output: (1 1), (1 2), (1 3), (2 1), (2 2), (2 3), (3 1), (3 2), (3 3) Think about and implement an iterative algorithm for the same task.

3. Write a program to generate and print all combinations with duplicates of k elements from a set with n elements. Sample input: n = 3 k = 2 Sample output: (1 1), (1 2), (1 3), (2 2), (2 3), (3 3) Think about and implement an iterative algorithm for the same task.

4. You are given a set of strings. Write a recursive program, which generates all subsets, consisting exactly k strings chosen among the elements of this set. Sample input: strings = {'test', 'rock', 'fun'} k = 2 Sample output: (test rock), (test fun), (rock fun) Think about and implement an iterative algorithm as well

Chapter Eight

Application of Graphical User Interface

In this chapter, we are going to transform our programs from just texts to a graphical interface which will look more appealing and interesting as compared to a line full of codes. In this section, the programmer is free to create images of various shapes as much as they can desire. The creation of interface requires well planning and use of intelligence to be able to express and output appealing products to the end line of the user.

The importance of graphics is that it is able to compress tasks and visualize a massive amount of written codes into an appealing work of art. In other words, the graphical interface makes work easier for the end user to interact with a program and understand the working concept of the whole program in a very short period of time. The picture below is a snippet of the early works of a graphic interface;

Some of the programs that enable the programmer to achieve such high graphical properties include; CAD- Computer Aided Design and CAM- Computer Aided Manufacturing. In this topic we are going to discuss how to incorporate the hardware and software part of graphics in C# programming language to achieve complex programs

The Graphical Hardware and Software

The Graphic Hardware

In modern technology, computers utilize the concept of a **bitmapped display** to output the products of most programs. In other words, the bit-mapped display consists of a screen which is made up of millions of pixels and picture elements. These pixels are usually laid out in a 2-Dimensional grid that can hold up to a range of (800-1560) x (600-1280). These are the numbers of the pixels in the 2-Dimensional grid. The quality of the display can be determined by the number of pixel in the output of the screen. Large numbers of pixels refer to high resolution whereas low numbers of pixels in a screen refer to low resolution. High-resolution images provide very clear and sharp pictures and low-resolution images provide less quality pictures which are sometimes blurry and less visible to the eyes.

In terms of storage components, the frame that stores the images in the actual screen is referred to as **buffer frames.** In connection to high-resolution pictures, the buffer frames required are directly related to the number of pixels that are found in the screen. However, a major drawback to the graphics technology is that the higher the resolution the more the memory required in the buffer frames of the screen. This main disadvantage here is that it requires almost four times the number of memory space that could have been used to store the program in text form.

The hardware which provides the display represents every value of the number of pixel in the buffer frame. It works by balancing the three colors which are Red, Blue and Green. The most interesting thing is that the balancing occurs for each and every pixel on the screen regardless of the range of numbers between half a million to two million pixels. It is also important to know that the color intensity of each and every pixel is not permanent but fades away within a fraction of a second.

For stability of a picture, repainting of the pixel is done quickly after the fading of the color intensity in order to avoid flickering of pictures. For these to be accurately achieved, the screen must be well updated and in good condition. The screen should also be refreshed at least thirty to fifty times a second. The user is also at the liberty of editing the balancing of the colors in order to achieve various shed of colors from the pixels. The shapes of images can also be altered by the modification of color intensity of the pixels

In summary, this is the fundamental concept of how the hardware part of the graphical usage operates in order to produce graphical images. In the next subtopic we are now going to discuss the software part of graphical programming.

Graphical software

In this study, we are going to focus on the software part of setting of pixels until a clear image is achieved. We are going to have a deeper understanding of functions from the graphic library that helps in controlling the settings and clearance of the graphical pixels.

In C# programming language, the graphic library that is involved in graphical software is very powerful. The extensive graphic library can be used to create complex figures, shapes, images and very clear pictures. Some of the complex operations that can be achieved in C# programming language include the drawing of geometric figures and shapes, creation of scrolling interfaces, creation of buttons and also menus that pull down.

We are going to get into further studies on how to create C# graphics using Visual Studio program.

Begin with a Windows Form App project. A window called **"Form 1"**will appear on the screen. This is done by the IDE of the C# programming language. It is done automatically but the learner must know that there were a lot of codes that were generated before the automatic creation of the form. The form appears as shown below;

If the student is interested to see the lines of codes that were used to generate the form he or she can click on the <> buttons in the windows form. The following lines of code should appear;

```
using System;
using System.Collections.Generic;
using System.ComponentModel;
using System.Data;
using System.Drawing;
using System.Linq;
using System.Text;
using System.Threading.Tasks;
using System.Windows.Forms;
```

```
namespace GraphicsProgram
{
public partial class Form1 : Form
{
public Form1()
{
InitializeComponent();
}
}
}
```

Secondly, we want to draw a basic line in the form created above and see the lines of codes that are used to generate the lines in graphical form. We will draw the simple line from point A (21, 21) to point B (101,101). The diagram below shows the illustration;

The line of code that is used to generate the graphic is as shown below;

```
public Form1()
{ //This is the  form on which drawing will appear
InitializeComponent(); // initialization of the form
this.Text = "C# Graphics";
Graphics drawingCanvas = CreateGraphics();
Show();
Pen BlackPen = new Pen(Color.Black, 2);
drawingCanvas.DrawLine
(BlackPen, 21, 21, 101, 101);
}
```

Understanding our code

The first line of the statement of the code calls the initialization of the element function. The function is used to automatically generate the form. The second line of statement displays the texts that will appear on the title bar of the window. The third line of statement produces the platform where the line is drawn or the background surface of the form. The line of the statement containing **"Show ();"** enables the form to be shown on the screen.

"Pen BlackPen = new Pen(Color.Black, 2);"is the piece of code that creates the pen that will paint the line on the form.

Practical Exercise

1. Run the following code and note the changes that will occur and the new things that you can observe;

    i. ```
        public Form1()
        { // This is the form on which drawing will appear
        InitializeComponent(); // initialization of the form
        this.Text = "C# Graphics";
        Graphics drawingCanvas = CreateGraphics();
        Show();
        Pen BlackPen = new Pen(Color.Black, 2);
        drawingCanvas.DrawARectangle
        (BlackPen, 26, 61, 51, 41);
        }
        ```

    ii. ```
        public Form1()
        { //This the form on which drawing will appear
        InitializeComponent(); // initialization of the form
        this.Text = "C# Graphics";
        Graphics drawingCanvas = CreateGraphics();
        Show();
        ```

```
Pen BlackPen = new Pen(Color.Black, 2);
drawingCanvas.DrawEllipse
(BlackPen,-24, 26, 126, 126);
}
```

iii. public Form1()
```
{ // This is the form on which drawing will appear
InitializeComponent(); // initialization of the form
this.Text = "C# Graphics";
Graphics drawingCanvas = CreateGraphics();
Show();
Pen BlackPen = new Pen(Color.Black, 2);
drawingCanvas.DrawEllipse
(BlackPen,-20, 20, 120, 120);
}
```

iv. public Form1()
```
{ // This isform on which drawing will occur
InitializeComponent(); // initialize form
this.Text = "C# Graphics";
Graphics drawingCanvas = CreateGraphics();
Show();
Pen BlackPen = new Pen(Color.Black, 2);
drawingCanvas.DrawRectangle
(BlackPen, 90, 90, 40, 90);
Brush redBrush = Brushes.Red;
Font f = new Font("Consolas", 12);
drawingCanvas.DrawString
("Stop", f, redBrush,100, 130);
}
```

Enabling a Mouse and other operations

In order for the mouse to be enabled to click in the C# programming language, an event handler must be initiated in the windows form. This is a piece of code that is able to sense an activity and hence react to the activity.

The program below illustrates the use of Mouse Clicks in a newly created form;

```
private void Form1_MouseClick
(object sender, MouseEventArgs e)
{
int x;
int y;
x = e.X;
y = e.Y;
if((x >= 90) && (x <= 140) &&
(y >= 90) && (y <= 190))
{
MessageBox.Show("User clicked inside" +
" the button");
}
else
{
MessageBox.Show("User clicked outside" +
" the button");
}
}
```

Understanding our code

After the mouse has been enabled, the cursor that is displayed in the form is used to click on to the imaginary created rectangle and hence respond by outputting some feedback message as shown below;

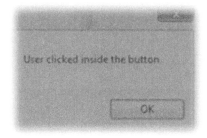

In summary, the knowledge shown above is a simple illustration of a real graphical interface both in hardware and software part. I hope you have understood a simple concept of GUI in C# programming language. Graphical programming enables us to create interesting pictures, objects and images that make programming to be very interesting and fun to engage in.

The following are some of the visual components

- A Form which is used to output the window.

- A Button which is used to output a clickable surface or button.

- A Textbox which is used to output a surface that can be edited.

- A Label which is used to output labels to other objects.

- A radiobutton which is used to output a selectable surface or button.

Chapter Nine

Basic Introduction of Lambda Expression

In this short chapter, we are going to study some powerful capabilities of C# programming language which includes the use of lambda expressions.

Lambda expressions are used in addition of functionality to classes. They are defined as anonymous functions which are used as expressions. The entire lambda operators use "=>" which is read as goes to. In C# programming language, the left side of the sequence of operators is for the input parameters while the right side is used for expressions that manipulate the input parameters.

Lambda expressions are usually applied as predicates rather than the delegates. The example below is used for learning of the lambda operators;

```
List<int> list = new List<int>() { 2, 3, 4, 5, 6, 7 };
List<int> evenNumbers = list.FindAll(x => (x % 2) == 0);
foreach (var num in evenNumbers)
{
Console.Write("{0} ", num);
}
Console.WriteLine();
```

Understanding our code

The example above is used to take the integer numbers that exist between 2 and 7 which are even. The process is achieved by the use of a lambda method that sorts out the even numbers. A looping system is used where all of the numbers that are listed above are checked if it's a multiple of two. The Boolean expression that is used is **(x % 2) == 0**).

In order to deeply understand the use of lambda expression, we are going to use another example containing the lambda expression and the extension method.

```
class Puppy
{
public string Name { get; set; }
public int Age { get; set; }
}
static void Main()
{
List<Puppy> puppies = new List<Puppy>() {
new Puppy { Name = "Tex", Age = 2 },
new Puppy { Name = "Dean", Age = 0 },
new Puppy { Name = "Tracy", Age = 2 }
};
var names = puppies.Select(x => x.Name);
foreach (var name in names)
{
Console.WriteLine(name);
}

}
```

Understanding our code;

The example above shows a collection of data obtained from a particular class. We use the extension method select () to obtain the list of all the names of the dogs. It is important to note that the keyword "var" is used to command the compiler to check out the type of variables depending on the return value from the right side.

Body of Lambda Expressions

In this subtopic we will consider the body of lambda functions and the statements that are found in the body of the function.

The example below will illustrate the body of the function;

```
List<int> list = new List<int>() { 22, 3, 7, 9, 6, 50 };
// This will process each and every argument having code statements
var evenNumbers = list.FindAll((i) =>
{
Console.WriteLine("The value of i is: {0}", i);
return (i % 2) == 0;
});
```

The result that will be obtained by running the code will be;

```
The value of i is: 22
The value of i is: 3
The value of i is: 7
The value of i is: 9
The value of i is: 6
The value of i is: 50
```

Understanding our code

The example above is the example of the even numbers program using the lambda expression. It is used to illustrate the possibility of printing through the console about the values of numbers worked upon by the body of the lambda function. The return value will evaluate whether the number is either even or odd integer value.

Practical Exercise

1. Implement the following extension methods for the classes, implementing

   the interface **IEnumerable<T>**: **Sum()**, **Min()**, **Max()**, **Average()**.

2. Evaluate and research about the following piece of code that applies the lambda expression;

   ```
   Class Form1:Form{
   private System.Windows.Forms.Button button1;
   ///...
   Void init(){
   // the arguments a,b are just to satisfy the delegate signature.
   // they do nothing useful in this simple example.
   this.button1.Click += (a,b) => { this.button1.Text = "clicked1"; };
   }
   }
   ```

Chapter Ten

Object-Oriented Programming

Introduction

We have learned about various techniques that are used in conquering big tasks and breaking down to smaller tasks hence an easier solution to programming. Some of the techniques were subroutine programming and also the divide and conquer techniques.

On the other end, object-oriented programming uses a different approach to solving problems. A program is seen as a blueprint of another part of the world which becomes the common place of interest. The common place of interest in this world is the objects. Hence we shall look deeper into this world of view and see how C# programming language has manipulated this type of programming.

Introduction to classes, objects and namespaces

Classes are a model containing actual objects and entities. The characteristics of the class are known as their properties. The behavior of the class is known as the method of the class. The behavior and characteristic of the class are visible within the enclosure of the class which can either be declared private or public. In summary the objects can be defined as an instance of a class

In this type of programming, a class can contain very many other subtasks inside it. In solving these smaller tasks, the objects assist in solving a section or two. It provides the services that are linked in total solving of the whole task.

In an OOP when the program is executed, various objects are requested to perform a service and hence they are expected to manipulate the situation and return a result. Once a result is returned, the allocated subtask is considered as solved by the object. It is very important to know that an object works as an independent entity. This is because it has its own values that it manipulates during a service request.

A new feature with objects is that it works on behalf of the classes. When a class is supposed to carry out a subtask or a function, the object that is found in that class will perform the function on its behalf.

There are several terms and features that are associated with object-oriented programming but we are going to discuss them later in the chapter. These terms include; inheritance, abstraction, encapsulation and polymorphism.

Before that let us get to understand the relationship between OOP and C# programming language

Relationship between C sharp programming language and OOP

The questions that should be running in our heads include; how do we incorporate two programming technique into real programs? How do they become one? It is vital to understand that not all the programming languages are compatible with object-oriented programming but the C# programming language is very much compatible.

In other words, the C# programming language is an object-oriented programming in itself. This is because the lines of codes are enclosed inside a class. The example below is a nice illustration;

```
class TravelOrganiser
{
//This is theMain function
}
```

For instance, when a class is written, various properties are specified such as the variables and the functions which the object of the same class can manipulate. Let's examine the program below and see some of these components;

```
//This the program that helps the GamingWorld to estimate their costs
//Written by M. Brown, 1/2/18
using System;
namespace GamingWorld
{
class Circle

{
private const double pi = 3.1416;
private double radius;
public void setRadius(double value)
//initializes the radius equal to value
{
radius = value;
}
public double getRadius()
//returns the current radius
{
return radius;
}
public double doCircumference()
```

```csharp
//Calculates and returns the circumference of a circle
{
return 2 * pi * radius;
}
public double doArea()
//Calculates and returns the area of a circle
{
return pi * radius * radius;
}
}
class Program
{
static void getInput(ref double newRadius, ref char taskToDo)
//Finds the radius and choice of manipulation by the user
{
Console.WriteLine();
Console.Write("Enter the value of the radius of a " +
"pool: ");
newRadius = Convert.ToDouble(Console.ReadLine());
//Oversees what user wants to calculate
Console.WriteLine("Input your choice of task.");
Console.Write("C to compute circumference, " +
"A to compute area: ");
taskToDo = Convert.ToChar(Console.ReadLine());
}
static void Main(string[] args)
{
double newRadius = 0; // the radius of the pool
char taskToDo = ' '; //it holds the user choice to compute circumference
or area
char more; //controls loop for
//helps in processing more pools
Circle swimmingPool = new Circle();

Console.Write("Do you want to process a pool? (Y or N): ");
more = Convert.ToChar(Console.ReadLine());
```

```
while (more == 'Y') //provides more circles to process
{
getInput(ref newRadius, ref taskToDo);
swimmingPool.setRadius(newRadius);
if (taskToDo == 'C') //calculates the circumference
{
Console.WriteLine("The circumference for a pool " +
"of radius " +
swimmingPool.getRadius().ToString("##.##") +
" is " +
swimmingPool.doCircumference().ToString
("##.##"));
}
else //compute area
{
Console.WriteLine("The area for a pool " +
"of radius " +
swimmingPool.getRadius().ToString("##.##") +
" is " +
swimmingPool.doArea().ToString("##.##"));
}
Console.WriteLine();
Console.Write("Do you want to process more pools? " +
"(Y or N): ");
more = Convert.ToChar(Console.ReadLine());
} //end of while loop
//finish up
Console.WriteLine("Program will now terminate.");
}
}
}
```

Understanding our code

The example above is a long piece of code that I expect us to follow keenly. A circle object can be best defined by considering its radius.

By the use of the radius we can calculate two things; circumference and area. In order to achieve this mathematical function, we need to establish the value of the pi and specify it in a class.

Therefore, in the circle class, the variables are pi and the radius of the specific circle. The functions in this class include setRadius, doArea, and doCircumference among others. The members of the class are Main and getInput.

The main disturbing question is: How do the two classes work together? The best answer to give is that if one class wants to communicate to the other it must declare an object that exists in that other class. The following code shows how it all happens;

```
Console.WriteLine("The circumference for the pool " +
"of radius " +
swimmingPool.getRadius().ToString("##.##") +
" is " +
swimmingPool.doCircumference().ToString
("##.##"));
```

Understanding our code

The declaration of the object from the class Circle is called from the swimmingpool. This means that the swimmingpool can call from the other class too.

The statements inquire from the swimmingpool to call the function getRadius and later to manipulate the function doCircumference. To the swimmingpool the circle class appears to be an instance.

Before we get to the features in the object-oriented programming I would like the student to go through another long piece of code and try to go through the various features and do a small research on it as an assignment;

Practical exercise

1. Study the following program keenly and evaluate yourself on the relationship between OOP and C#.

```
using System;
namespace Shapes
{
public class Circle
{
const double pi = 3.1416;
private double radius;
public void setRadius(double value)
{ //sets radius of the circle equal to value
radius = value;
}
public double getRadius()
{ //return radius
return radius;
}
public double doArea()
{ //computes and writes out area of the circle
return pi * radius * radius;
}
}
public class Rectangle
{
protected double width;
protected double height;
public void setWidth(double value)
{ //sets width of rectangle equal to value
width = value;
```

```
}
public void setHeight(double value)
{ //sets height of rectangle equal to value
height = value;
}
public double getWidth()
{ //returns width
return width;
}

public double getHeight()
{ //returns height
return height;
}
public double doArea()
{ //computes and writes out area of the rectangle
return width * height;
}
}
public class Square
{
private double side;
public void setSide(double value)
{ //sets the side of the square equal to value
side = value;
}
public double getSide()
{ //returns side
return side;
}
public double doArea()
{ //computes and writes out the area of the square
return side * side;
}
}
public class Square2 : Rectangle
```

```
//Square is derived class of Rectangle,
//uses the inherited height and width
//properties and the inherited doArea function
{
public void setSide(double value)
{ //sets the side of the square equal to value
height = value;
width = value;
}
public double getSide()
{ //returns side (width)
return width;
}
}
class Program
{
static void Main(string[] args)
{
Circle joe = new Circle();
joe.setRadius(23.5);

Console.WriteLine("The area of a circle with "
+ "radius " + joe.getRadius() + " is "
+ joe.doArea());
Rectangle luis = new Rectangle();
luis.setWidth(12.4);
luis.setHeight(18.1);
Console.WriteLine("The area of a rectangle with "
+ "dimensions " + luis.getWidth() + " and "
+ luis.getHeight() + " is " + luis.doArea());
Square anastasia = new Square();
anastasia.setSide(3);
Console.WriteLine("The area of a square with "
+ "side " + anastasia.getSide() + " is "
+ anastasia.doArea());
Square2 tyler = new Square2();
```

```
tyler.setSide(4.2);
Console.WriteLine("The area of a square with "
+ "side " + tyler.getSide() + " is "
+ tyler.doArea());
    }
}
}
```

2. What is the output from the following section of code if it is added to the Main function of the C# program?

```
Square one = new Square();
one.setSide(10);
Console.WriteLine("The area of a square with "
+ "side " + one.getSide() + " is "
+ one.doArea());
```

Please go through the lines of codes as an assignment and do intense research in order to evaluate yourself whether you have understood the relationship between object-oriented programming and C# programming language.

Definition and fundamental principles (Inheritance, Abstraction, Polymorphism and Encapsulation)

These are the fundamental principles that define the Object-oriented programming. They create the basis of links and relationship to the classes and objects in the C# programming language. Let's give a summary introduction of these fundamental principles before we study each of them independently together with their examples;

- **Inheritance-** this is briefly used in a class hierarchy to advance code reusability and readability.

- **Abstraction-** this is used to consider important properties of objects while ignoring other minor properties.

- **Polymorphism-** this is used to incorporate different objects to work together with consideration of an abstract behavior.

- **Encapsulation-** this is used in hiding of unnecessary details of the classes hence create a simple structure that is clear and neat.

Inheritance

From the word inherit; a class takes characteristics of another class. For example, a tiger belongs to a biological class of cats. Hence it will have characteristics like the hunting of prey and having four paws. These characteristics can also be used in a class of lions, cheetahs and puma.

Inheritance works with Dot Net framework in C# programming language. This is done by declaring a class using a special construct. However, the C# programming language and other modern languages only allow single inheritance of a class from another class. The other older programming languages such as C++ could allow multiple inheritances of classes. This was later discovered to be a great disadvantage because of confusion of inheritance from different methods. The main class which characteristics are inherited from is known as **parent class** while the class that inherits is called the **super/ child or base class.**

The following is an example that shows inheritance;

1. The super or base class;

```
/// <summary>Felidae is latin for "cats"</summary>
public class Felidae
{
private bool male;
// This constructor calls another constructor
public Felidae() : this(true)
{}
// This is the constructor that is inherited
public Felidae(bool male)
{
this.male = male;
}
public bool Male
{

get { return male; }
set { this.male = value; }
}
}
```

2. the parent class;

```
public class Lion : Felidae
{
private int weight;
// Keyword "base" will be explained in the next paragraph
public Lion(bool male, int weight) : base(male)
{
this.weight = weight;
}
public int Weight
{
get { return weight; }
```

```
set { this.weight = value; }
    }
}
```

In summary, the keyword "base" is used for the purpose of clarity. It invokes the method from the super class. The advantage of this operation is that it makes it easier to read so that we can know from which method the inheritance was made from.

Abstraction

In deep definition, abstraction means manipulating an entity that we assume we know it but in the real sense we do not know how it internally operates. This is a principle that is practiced on a daily basis. For example, we used this principle in graphical programming where we use objects without understanding the internal operation of figures. There are so many examples of abstraction but the best thing is to learn how to apply it in C# programming language.

Some of the major uses of abstraction include; writing of codes that work best in the environment of abstract data structures. I hope we remember examples of abstract data structures such as arrays, dictionaries and lists. For example we can decide to save data values into the list without getting concerned if they were arranged and organized in arrays or not.

In summary, abstraction creates an interface that can be used by other applications. This can be incorporated by the subdivision of abstract data into small sub-data that creates flexibility in working with smaller programs. The small programs are called **components.** This criterion of writing component programs is widely used since it allows for reuse of objects and line of codes

The following is a program that incorporates the use of abstraction. Study it carefully;

```
public class AbstractionExample
{
static void Main()
{
Lion lion = new Lion(true, 150);
Felidae bigCat1 = lion;
AfricanLion africanLion = new AfricanLion(true, 80);
Felidae bigCat2 = africanLion;
}
}
```

Encapsulation

This fundamental principle is also known as information hiding. The object is entitled to provide the users with the necessary information without other details. The necessary details are those that are going to be manipulated by the programmer.

For example, using a computer's keyboard, screen and mouse without minding of how they are interconnected and the components that power them in order to work successfully. Therefore in the program, the unnecessary details in the methods are hidden whereas the essential properties to be manipulated are displayed.

The following is an example of how encapsulation is done;

```
public class Lion : Felidae, Reproducible<Lion>
{
// ...
private Paw frontLeft;
private Paw frontRight;
private Paw bottomLeft;
```

```
private Paw bottomRight;
private void MovePaw(Paw paw) {
// ...
}
public override void Walk()
{
this.MovePaw(frontLeft);
this.MovePaw(frontRight);
this.MovePaw(bottomLeft);
this.MovePaw(bottomRight);
}
// ...
}
```

Understanding our code

The example above helps us to learn about hiding methods that the user of the class will not use hence will not be necessary to display. The tiger privately hides other details about their movements which is called encapsulation of behavior.

Polymorphism

In order to have a deeper understanding of this fundamental principle we have to look at it from a different perspective. Polymorphism is the treating of data objects of a derived class that is the same as the object of the super or child class.

It bears strong similarities to abstraction but its major function includes an override of a method most especially from the derived class. This is done in order to alter the initial behavior or characteristic of the derived class.

Practical Exercises

1. We are given a **school**. The school has classes of students. Each class has a set of **teachers**. Each teacher teaches a set of **courses**. The students have a name and a unique number in the class. **Classes** have a unique text identifier. Teachers have names. Courses have a name, count of classes and count of exercises. The teachers as well as the students are people. Your task is to model the classes (in terms of OOP) along with their attributes and operations define the class hierarchy and create a class diagram with Visual Studio.

2. Implement the following classes: **Dog**, **Frog**, **Cat**, **Kitten** and **Tomcat**. All of them are animals (**Animal**). Animals are characterized by **age**, **name** and **gender**. Each animal makes a sound (use a virtual method in the **Animal** class). Create an array of different animals and print on the console their name, age and the corresponding sound each one makes.

Chapter Eleven

Summary and Conclusion

I would like to congratulate you for the patience and determination that you have reached this far with the C# programming language. I also hope you have equipped yourself with various skills about different principles that can be applied even in other programming languages.

As the years pass by, the technologies will change and the programming languages will change their structures and techniques. However, the fundamental knowledge of the data algorithm and structures will be the skeleton that will steer the advancements. This shows you of the importance of learning these basic skills in the current programming language.

Have you solved all the problems?

I can call proudly call you a programmer if you have carefully gone through all the examples and the practical exercises and you have understood the various techniques that are implemented in the C# programming language.

At this point you are able to play about with any technology because they share concepts and fundamental principles. This is a great vantage point over other programmers because you know the use of data structures such as the hash tables and lists. This is a level where you can also teach other people about the programming concept in general with a lot of confidence. The knowledge you have acquired in this book will help you through the years to develop your skill in programming.

I would also like to refer you to other sources if there is a point where you did not understand. There are millions of resources on the internet that complement each other and hence feel free to refer. You can also watch videos about the same.

What next after this book?

You might be stranded on the next step to take after exhausting the study of this book. I want to assure you that you have the best foundation of software engineering hence you are good to develop yourself further. I would also like to prescribe to you the following counsels;

1. **Pick a programming language with a corresponding framework or platform.** A good example of such is the one we have studies in the book of C# and Dot Net platform. Other platforms include; Java language with Java EE, PHP with CakePHP, Ruby with Rails and many others. do not feel tied to the C# programming language; you can also explore other programming languages.

2. **Find resources and books about databases**. This will enable you to create complex applications using tables and relations. Learn about the queries, Oracle, MySQL and ORM technologies.

3. **Research about the creation of dynamic websites**. This can help you in creating web applications for mobile phones and devices. Examples are HTML, JavaScript, CSS and JQuery.

4. **Acquire materials on how to build mobile applications**. This is an economic opportunity where you can create applications that can be bought and maintained by Apple, Amazon, Google and Microsoft. Programs like Cordova and HTML5 are good for such development. This will expose you to the latest technologies and hence open your bright future with programming.

5. **Engage in serious programming projects**. Serious programming projects include the creation of web marketing programs, accounting programs, performance analysis software among others. This will expose you to the real world where there are more practical problems as compared to the basic examples in the book. You will be able to gain experience which is practical and timelier.

6. **Find a job in a software or programming company**. This is an important practical opportunity. A job offer will come if you are sharp and efficient in solving problems in society using the lines of codes. I believe that the examples in this book have opened your thoughts and expanded your experience in coding. The secret to self-development is to not only seek for jobs but also volunteer if there are no jobs. In this way you will learn about new software technologies, interact with different programming techniques and also get to work with other programmer teams. You will come to appreciate later about the

beauty of learning about data structures and other techniques of C# programming.

7. **PRACTICE EVERY DAY!** This is a tool that people are advised in order to grasp complex concepts. If you talk and listen from successful programmers and software engineers they will advise you about two things; practice every day and go an extra mile out of your daily practice. This means that by practicing every day you will learn of the things you have been overlooking and also you will understand some of the hard concepts that people find challenging. Secondly, going an extra mile means putting more efforts into doing research on a daily basis. This can be by looking on the internet, watching videos about programming, challenging your team members about a concept and many other techniques. This will help you to grow at a very fast rate and become a genius of programming within a very short time.

8. **I WISH YOU THE BEST IN YOUR PROGRAMMING CAREER!**

Printed in Great Britain
by Amazon